which?
essential guides

KT-409-720

BUY, SELL AND MOVE HOUSE

KATE FAULKNER

This book is for my Dad, Professor Terry Faulkner.
He taught me that 'I can do it' and was always there if things were
going wrong. Without him, I wouldn't be where I am now.

Which? Books are commissioned and published by Which? Ltd,
2 Marylebone Road, London NW1 4DF
Email: books@which.co.uk

Distributed by Littlehampton Book Services Ltd, Faraday Close, Durrington,
Worthing, West Sussex BN13 3RB

British Library Cataloguing in Publication Data
A catalogue record for this book is available from the British Library

ISBN 1 84490 026 6 / 978 184490 026 8

Although the author and publishers endeavour to make sure the information
in this book is accurate and up-to-date, it is only a general guide. Before taking
action on financial, legal, or medical matters you should consult a qualified
professional adviser, who can consider your individual circumstances. The author
and publishers can not accordingly accept liability for any loss or damage
suffered as a consequence of relying on the information contained in this guide.

Author's acknowledgements
My thanks go to Sean and Emma Callery, Bob Vickers, Jenni Conti, Melanie
Green, Dermott Jewell, Mike Naylor, Louise Restell, Pete Tynan, Ian Robinson
and Angela Newton; Mark Spurling at RBS Associates; Karen Babington at
Easier 2 Move; Tom McClelland at McClelland Slater; Sarah McShane at RICS
and Vanessa Ambler at Inspectorhome.

Additional text by: Sean Callery
Cover photographs by: Getty/Photolibrary
Printed and bound by Scotprint, Scotland

For a full list of Which? Books, please call 01903 828557, access our
website at www.which.co.uk, or write to Littlehampton Book Services.
For other enquiries call 0800 252 100.

which?
essential guides

BUY, SELL
AND MOVE
HOUSE

66 Buying and selling property is a complex and stressful experience; no matter how many times you do it, there will always be new things to consider.**99**

Kate Faulkner

About the author

Kate Faulkner has bought and renovated properties for many years and has now worked in the property industry for over seven years, both as an adviser to relocating companies and individual consumers. She runs a website called designsonproperty.co.uk, and is currently head of marketing for a self-build and renovation company. The author of two previous property books, Kate provides help to people buying and selling property throughout the UK.

Contents

Introduction

Buying or selling property is one of the most stressful events in your life, ranking right up there with divorce and bereavement. It involves taking momentous decisions about your finances and lifestyle as you travel on a rollercoaster of emotions from the excitement of finding somewhere you'd love to live in, to the horrible realisation that you might not get it.

In the UK and Ireland we have a love/hate relationship with property: we value property owning more highly than our European neighbours and we delight in discussing the seemingly inexorable rise in prices. While we regret the difficulties young people have in buying the smallest bedsit, we rejoice in the bonanza made possible by selling a large home to help finance a retirement. We shudder at the horror stories of gazumping, greed and incompetence, but hope ourselves to 'buy low, sell high'.

Yet every estate agent can tell a tale of a disingenuous vendor or a hopelessly naive buyer, and solicitors will assure you that the cause of many of the delays they are accused of are the deliberate slowness of clients looking for opportunities to make an extra bonus on their sale: the fact is, the property market brings out the worst in people.

YOUR PRIDE AND JOY

Buying or selling a home is an emotional as well as a financial decision. Many of our memories are tied up with our homes and it is part of human nature to identify ourselves in some way with where we live. We take pride in our homes and we resent the implied criticism of viewers who don't want to buy them.

So dealing in property plays with our emotions and takes us on a journey through the nightmare world of the property chain, where one person's prevarication can spell misery for many families. We enter the habitat of the estate agent, an unregulated business environment in which trust is a rare commodity. Which? has long campaigned for a decent system of regulation for estate agents, yet sadly anyone can set up as one, and while there are organisations with codes of conduct, many agents operate outside of their control.

THE SEVEN-YEAR TWITCH

Selling or buying a house is rarely straightforward, and doing both simultaneously is like a recipe for a nervous breakdown. But in an increasingly hectic, insecure job market where not being prepared to move can threaten your career, and an educational system where being in the catchment area for the right school is seen as essential, moving house is part of the modern world: on average we will move house every seven years.

Given that house selling and buying is notoriously stressful, what can you do to keep calm? This book will help by providing you with the essential information you need to sell and buy a house and stay sane. The first step is to accept, then ignore, your emotions: dealing in property calls for a rational mind. The biggest mistakes people tend to make are to over estimate what they need and what they can afford. As a result, they tend to view the wrong properties and make offers that they cannot possibly finance. And they can't even blame the estate agent for the resulting misery!

"Buying or selling a home is an emotional as well as a financial decision. Try to keep feelings in check as you travel the route to completion. "

GET REAL

Our view of what we can buy is likely to be heavily influenced by the low interest rates of recent years. But, just as property prices can fall as well as rise, so the cost of a mortgage can soar dramatically if the financial institutions get nervous about the future of the economy. Our watchwords as we look for mortgages should be 'affordability' and as we view property details it needs to be 'realism'. The guidance on mortgages stresses the importance of knowing what you really could afford in tougher times and resisting the lure of the big loan (see pages 24–37). If you can't pay it, the lender won't suffer: they'll get their money back by selling your property.

The key to property realism is to know the market, and not just as a buyer, but as a seller, too. The chapter on selling your property (pages 89–122) stresses the importance of researching your local property market. That way you'll price your property realistically (helping you to know what properties you can afford to view) and you'll choose a decent, local agent who is able to do a good job for you. There are rogue agents out there, but if you have a good understanding of the market, you are more likely to spot them and give them the wide berth they deserve.

With your research skills honed, you'll be ready to take on the role of buyer with confidence: knowing what you want, where you are likely to get it and how much it ought to cost.

A NEW HIP

Throughout both of these processes it is imperative that you stay highly organised, with your paperwork in order and a clear idea of what you need to do next. This is going to be especially important with the introduction in England and Wales (and later, Scotland) of Home Information Packs (HIPs) (see pages 105–8). This major change in property buying will put the onus on the seller to provide accurate, comprehensive information on their property. It ought to make buying a property easier and quicker, and reduce the astonishing failure rate that means a third of accepted offers come to nothing in the end. Other changes in practice, such as the key shift that makes stamp duty and registering the property the responsibility of the buyer (not their legal firm) are explained so that you can avoid any pitfalls.

One of the reasons property buying is so stressful is that you are (or feel you are) at the mercy of other people: agents, solicitors, surveyors, and other buyers and vendors in your chain. The guidance on managing the chain (see pages 155–62) shows how you can stay in control: armed with the right information, you really can do a lot to keep the chain moving and ensure that those removal lorries roll as they should on moving day. There is also advice on choosing and handling removals firms, utility providers and insurance companies (see pages 163–72).

Moving day itself can be highly traumatic, and this book offers advice on how you can prepare for it and survive it so that your first night in your new home feels like a honeymoon and not a wake.

The property buying process is different in Scotland, Northern Ireland and Ireland, and this book provides comprehensive explanations of the systems in those countries (see pages 183–92 and 193–203). Interspersed through the book are 'jargon buster' boxes explaining any technical terms, and there is also a comprehensive glossary on pages 204–7 and full contact details on pages 208–13.

With the help of this book you can ensure that searching for a dream home doesn't turn into a nightmare, and sleep safe in the knowledge that you are confident on how to take this major step in your life. Happy viewing!

❝ Use this book to ensure that searching for your dream home remains as positive an experience as possible. ❞

The property market

Property is big business, and nearly all of us get involved in the market sometime – with varying degrees of enthusiasm. This chapter gives an overview of the market, introduces the essential information and explains the likely timescales involved. It also explains the importance of new laws, which have a major impact on the process of buying and selling a home.

Moving facts and figures

Rises and falls in house prices regularly feature in news reports, and most newspapers (both national and local) run substantial specialist sections on the subject. Few dinner parties finish without some reference to it, from the amazing price paid for a shell of a building to the difficulty that young people have in affording even the smallest place of their own.

However, there is much hype about the property market and when you are buying and selling a property it is hard to get to grips with the essential facts and figures that help to equip you for a successful move. The following information puts the house market in context and helps you to plan your move from the start.

Key figures often quoted by the media include:

- The average price of a home.
- The number of properties sold in any year.
- Whether the market is increasing or decreasing.
- Regional variations.

At any one time there are 300,000–375,000 properties on the market, and they'll be on the books for an

❝At any one time there are 300,000–375,000 properties on the market, and they'll be on the books for an average of three months each. ❞

average of three months each. Recently the market has stabilised after some years when it was quite possible for the value of your home to rise by more than many people's annual salary. The previous price differential between the south east and the rest of the UK has also closed in recent years as prices have stabilised or gone down while they have carried on increasing in much of the rest of the country.

 You can find current data on moving facts at these websites: www.landregistry.gov.uk; www.hometrack.co.uk and www.rics.org. There is also additional information on relevant pages throughout this book.

New homes

Nearly 155,000 new homes were built in the financial year ending 31 March 2005, a 6 per cent rise on the previous year and the third consecutive year when the figure has gone up. More than 500 newly built homes are purchased every day throughout the year in the UK, and the number of new houses being built has risen significantly since the start of this millennium.

We move house on average every seven years, which is obviously when most of us take an active interest in the market, but like it or not, all home owners need the property market to stay healthy. For this to happen, we are reliant on a steady flow of first-time buyers to fuel the market in the first place. So when you are looking to buy or sell a property, it is crucial to understand whether first-time buyers are active as they will influence the market in general. It is also essential to understand your local property market, as this will impact on your move (see Chapter 3, pages 79–82).

FIRST-TIME BUYERS

First-time buyers have traditionally been vital to the health of the property market because they are the start of nearly every chain of purchases. A number of factors have made it increasingly difficult for first-time buyers to get on the first rung of the property ladder:

- **House prices** have risen faster than wages, putting more properties out of their range.
- The abolition of **tax relief** on mortgages in 2000 increased the real cost of a mortgage.
- Many **graduates** leave university with a hefty student loan to repay, reducing the amount of money they have available for property.
- **Property investors** have continued to snap up similar properties to first-time buyers, pricing them out of the market.

As a result, the average age of the first-time buyer has risen to 34 years. An average of £120,000–150,000 is spent on a first house or flat, and it takes just under five years to save up the 5 per cent **deposit**. First-time buyers have increasingly opted to:

- **Accept financial help** from their family towards their deposits
- Use their **parents** as **guarantors** on the loan.
- **Share mortgages,** sometimes with

Jargon buster

Deposit The down payment
Guarantor Person who will guarantee to pay on your behalf should you be unable to repay a loan
Shared ownership Scheme where a housing association helps in the purchase of a property

as many as four people contributing to a purchase.
- **Opt for cheaper,** smaller properties with little or no garden.
- **Go to lenders** prepared to offer first-time buyers 100 per cent mortgages.

Increasingly, those that are eligible also have access to 'shared ownership' homes, which are being built in local areas by housing associations.

Because they are so crucial to the state of the property market, it is worth researching into first-time buyers when you value your property. If there are plenty of first-time buyers, the market is buoyant. A shortage of them quietens the market.

TYPES OF PROPERTY

Just driving around the UK and looking at the houses on the roadside reveals the wide range of house styles that have been built over the centuries, sometimes nestling side by side. There really is something to suit everybody (although it might not necessarily be on the market in the right location at the right price at the right time when you are looking for it!). Older, 'character' properties with unusual features are especially popular and in short supply, so they command a higher price.

Thinking about the type (or types) of property you are looking to buy is an important decision. Some properties sell more quickly than others as they are in short supply. All properties, old or new, have advantages and disadvantages. Some people spend months searching for a type of property only to find that it doesn't exist in the area they are looking in or that it is way beyond what they can afford, or other people's offers get accepted first as they are cash buyers.

> **❝First-time buyers are vital to the health of the property market because they are the start of nearly every chain.❞**

 For more information on the different types of property that are available see pages 125–6. Each property has their advantages and disadvantages and it is up to you to decide what you want from your new home.

Essentials of moving home

Exciting, stressful, expensive, life-affirming, worrying, exhausting ... the list of adjectives people use to describe moving house is long and often contradictory. Without careful planning and an understanding of your own property market, it can be all of these things and more, so it is vital that you are sure you really want to do it.

A government survey discovered that an amazing third of all property buyers pull out of the purchase process after making an offer, often wreaking havoc on their own lives and on those of the sellers, buyer and (unpaid) agents up and down the **chain**.

REASONS TO MOVE

People move to new properties for many reasons, which generally boil down to a change in the required size of home or of location, or a change of lifestyle.

Space

New babies or new partners push the property market along. As people start living together, or start a family, or begin to work from home, they need more room. They might need more space for bedrooms, offices, storage for all their possessions or to improve their quality of life in some other way.

Jargon buster

Chain When there are more than two properties aiming to complete sale on the same day

Completion The final part of the transaction when the transfer of the property title is legally given to the new owner

Exchange of contracts A binding legal agreement that confirms the intention to transfer ownership of a property between a buyer and seller

Home Information Pack (HIP) From June 2007 it is mandatory to produce a pack of information about your property before putting it on the market (see pages 105–8)

Planning permission When permission has to be sought from the local council for changes to be made to a property

Sale contract Contract with an estate agent (see page 100)

Search Information on planning and environmental matters obtained from the local authority (see pages 147–8)

However, if you like where you live now, it is worth considering whether you would be able to extend your current home to provide the space you need with a new bathroom, bedroom or study. Maybe you can convert a loft into fresh living space or extend into your garden with a new living room or a conservatory? It is likely to be less stressful, and improving rather than moving gives you a chance to create the home of your dreams – but remember that your plans will be subject to **planning permission**.

> **❝ A third of all property buyers pull out of the purchase process after making an offer, affecting sellers and buyers up and down the chain. ❞**

Conversely, the other major reason why people move house is to downsize. The 'empty nesters' whose children have left home can find themselves rattling around a house that has too much space, and decide to downsize, freeing up equity to splash out on a cruise, safari or helping with the kids' education.

New job

Commuting is hard work on our congested roads and transport system, and many people would agree that a shorter daily journey time improves quality of life. So a new job further from home or in a completely different area may mean you have to move, or buy or rent somewhere to stay during the week. If you have the resources and take a job far away, renting a room or flat to stay in on weekdays can be a good compromise at first and a fine way to discover if you like the area you intend moving to.

New location needed

The debate between contrasting styles of town and country life has been going on for centuries. Some people live in one and yearn for the other, others wouldn't switch for the world, and the well-heeled have a home in each. Maybe you want to move locally to be nearer friends or family, or to be in the catchment area for a school you value. Similarly, divorce, separation or redundancy or bad luck can stimulate a move to a cheaper location or a smaller home. Perhaps you just fancy a change of scenery and culture. Britain is a wonderfully varied country with much to offer in every region. Sometimes people just need a change.

 The cost of moving is far from cheap. Chapter 2, starting on page 23, talks you through what is involved financially, both in the short-term (e.g. conveyancing, furniture movers) and the long-term (e.g. mortgage, running costs).

New style

Rightly or wrongly, for many of us, where we live represents who we are, and as we become more affluent, we want a home that reflects our station in life. An alternative is to renovate or redecorate – a new kitchen or bathroom, new doors or even just new door furniture can really lift the look of a home. All these options can transform a house and add to its value.

Time to get on the property ladder

UK property prices can rise at such a pace that for some people it feels like it is their last chance to own their own property. However, the government has published new draft planning guidelines to ensure that local authorities release more land to meet future requirements, and has committed itself to a 50 per cent increase in funding for social housing, aimed at delivering an extra 10,000 cheaper homes a year by 2007. So there should still be reasonably priced homes and flats for first-time buyers in the future – after all, the market needs them. Purchasing property is also a way to leave the family home or rented market. Many people still hold the view that property is a sound investment that could rise spectacularly in value and is very unlikely to fall. Unfortunately, property prices can go down as well as up.

REASONS NOT TO MOVE

Selling, buying and moving to a new property soaks up a lot of money, often in addition to the costs of a bigger mortgage. You may well need to save money in order to finance costs such as stamp duty, estate agents, solicitors and removals.

It is also easy to underestimate the emotional links you can feel with a house. It may be the place where you brought up children, or met your partner, or that has countless tiny connections that comfort you and make you feel part of it.

But the major reason to stay is that even the smoothest of house moves can be stressful and disruptive to the rhythm of your life. Bear in mind that changing where you live can be tiring in many ways: emotionally, mentally and physically – there's a lot to get through! If you can face that because what is at the other end of the road is worth it, then go ahead, but remember that the journey is rarely without hitches.

> **❝ It is easy to underestimate the emotional links you can feel with a house. It may be the place where you brought up children. ❞**

Finally, are you being realistic in your desire to move? It's only worth buying or moving if it will improve your quality of life. Have you got the funds or a likely selling price sufficient to buy what you want (for more information, see pages 24–35)?

The more you understand the issues you face, the easier it will be to overcome them, which is where this book is designed help.

❝ As a rough guide, the whole process of buying a house should take between three and six months. Buying and selling is likely to extend this to six to twelve months. ❞

HOW LONG WILL IT TAKE?

Many of us have heard horror stories of how long a house purchase can take, and amazing tales of very rapid successes. Key factors influencing the time span of buying and selling a house include the size of the chain and the state of the market (rising prices stimulate faster movement). The average time taken from starting to house hunt to exchanging contracts is now 22 weeks. A typical move can be broken down as follows:

- **From beginning to look to offer being accepted:** 12 weeks.
- **From offer acceptance to mortgage offer:** 4 weeks.
- **From mortgage offer to exchange of contracts:** 4 weeks.
- **From exchange of contracts to completion:** 2 weeks.

Remember that this is an average of completed sales (about 28 per cent never make it to completion) and there will be plenty that took less time and many that dragged on for month after month. In roughly one in ten cases it takes more than 20 weeks from agreeing an offer to exchanging contracts.

As a rough guide, then, the whole process of buying a house should take between three and six months. Buying

 The chain of events for selling and buying a property is lengthy. For an overview of both processes, see the flow charts on pages 18–19, which are designed to help you on your way.

Some 28 per cent of sales don't reach completion and approximately one in ten cases take more than 20 weeks from agreeing an offer to exchanging contracts. Take nothing for granted.

and selling is likely to extend this to six to twelve months (with the time to sell the average house being about five or more weeks). However, there are occasions when the whole process has been completed in as little as six weeks. That said, rapid movement involves quick decision making, which is not always best because we are not fully aware of all the implications of a decision, and feeling rushed into making important choices at this emotionally fragile time can be exceedingly stressful.

DECIDING TO MOVE

It can take some months for people to decide they want to move. This doesn't tend to be a smooth process as people may start looking for a property before they put their own up

❝ Putting your property up for sale should be a quick process, but Home Information Packs may extend the timescale. ❞

for sale, adding themselves to estate agent's mailing lists. They then either see a property they want, or decide that they are definitely going to move so put their home on the market. This process is frequently interrupted by other events – for example, someone might fall ill for a few weeks, be particularly busy at work, have another change in circumstance. As a result, they dip out of the market for a while, then come back in again at a later date, or drop out completely.

Putting your property up for sale

This should be a fairly quick process. The agent needs to take measurements of your home, which they often do when they come around to value your home. They may send someone around separately to take photos and do floor plans, and you need to agree the **contract of sale** and confirm the details that are produced on your behalf. However, the impact of the new **Home Information Packs** (see pages 105–8) may extend this process to a few weeks, depending on how quickly the new companies will provide them.

Selling a property

As a rough guide you can expect to receive an offer when ten people have viewed your home, which could take weeks or months. You may choose not to accept their first offer, and negotiations might continue for a week or so.

The property procedure

There's more to dealing in property than looking in agents' windows. The key phases are set out below. Sometimes two or more can be happening simultaneously, but it still helps to know where you are in the whole procedure, what happens next, and what you might have missed. All these stages are explained in detail on the pages stated.

Selling

Decide to move

Do you really want to? See page 90.

Carry out repairs

Get it looking its best. See pages 114-15.

Research the local market

Find out what your property might be worth. See pages 79-82.

Choose an agent

The right one will sell your home efficiently, or can you do it? See pages 95-100 and 103-4.

Select a legal representative

Have one on board for when you need them. See page 109.

HIP operational?

Prepare your Home Information Pack See pages 105-8.

Prepare your home

Clear clutter and create space. See page 115.

Market the property

Issue particulars and spread the word. See page 104.

Guide viewers

Don't say 'This is the lounge.' See pages 115-17.

Deal with offers

Is the buyer serious? See page 118.

Agree a price

What will you accept? See pages 86-8.

Conveyancing

Make it legal and agree what's included. See pages 110-11.

Exchange contracts

Finalise the sale. See pages 112-13.

Complete contracts

Start packing the lorry. See pages 161-2.

Buying

The affordability test

How much can you pay? See pages 24-35.

Map it out

Arrange a Mortgage Agreement in Principle. See page 40.

Choose your property type

What do you need? See pages 124-6.

Research the market

What's available, and what's selling? See pages 135-8.

Where?

Where are your property types? See pages 133-4.

Brief agents

Make your needs and wants clear. See pages 135-6.

Sort out a legal representative

Do it now so that you can move fast if need be. See page 109.

View properties

Could you live there? See pages 142-5.

Negotiate a price

What's it worth? See page 151.

Finalise your mortgage

Make sure you can afford it. See pages 36-56.

Survey

Get one done, or follow up on the HIP. See pages 152-3.

What's included?

Sort out fixtures and fittings. See page 111.

Conveyancing

Check all is well. See pages 159-60.

Who's going to move you?

Choose how you will move. See pages 164-7.

Exchange contracts

Now you're committed to the purchase. See pages 160-1.

Complete

Pay the money and move in. See pages 161-2.

Register your property

Make it yours and pay the stamp duty. See page 175.

Finding a property

Much depends here on how much you want to move, how realistic your expectations are and what is on the market. Having a buyer for your own property already is a powerful incentive for many to accept your offer rather than someone else's if it is a property much in demand.

Buying a property

The tasks of getting a survey done, arranging a mortgage on the property, carrying out legal searches and finalising the legal documents can overlap. But the time it takes to buy a property rests on many parties. You and the people selling the property need to get all the documentation ready quickly. The legal companies have to be ones that are happy to work to your deadlines, and the mortgage company will always want to know more information before they release tens of thousands of pounds to you. It is during this time that the HIPs should have beneficial impact as the searches will be done in advance and therefore cut down on the conveyancing process (see pages 105–8). The early searches should

also flush out any serious problems, which can be resolved before the property goes on to the market.

Chain pain

The length or complexity of the chain (i.e. how many people are linked together in a series of sales and purchases) is certainly a factor in the length of time that it takes to complete a sale, but a short chain can take ages if the people buying and selling, and the professionals involved, don't keep it moving.

The trouble with a chain is that everyone in it must exchange contracts on the same day, having completed all the legal and financial paperwork. This involves many people (conveyancers, estate agents, mortgage lenders, surveyors ...), most of whom you have no contact with (and no control over) because they're not working for you. You can influence this by making sure anyone acting for you is professional and efficient – and can work to deadlines you set, or even by approaching the task as a project and managing it yourself (see pages 103–4 and 111).

KEEPING THINGS MOVING

Whether you are buying, selling or both, there is a lot you can do to help keep things moving as fast as possible:

- **Specify a time frame** when agreeing the sale and purchase deals – then everyone knows what is required of them.

"When in a chain, everyone must exchange contracts on exactly the same day. You can influence this by making sure that everyone who is acting for you is professional and efficient."

- **Draw up draft sale contracts** when you put your property on the market.
- **Sort out your mortgage in principle** before looking for properties.
- **Fill in all information forms** as soon as you get them.
- **Book your surveyor** within a week of having an offer accepted, and ensure your legal company works as fast as possible.
- **Deliver paperwork** direct locally, and use a next-day delivery service for other written communication.
- **Specify a maximum of two weeks** between exchange and completion.
- **One or more of the parties** could agree to move to rented or temporary accommodation on a set date to free up a property in the chain, reducing the number of contracts to be exchanged on the same day.
- **Maintain a dialogue** with the estate agents along the chain – you can't speak to other people's legal representatives, but a good estate agent will be able to hurry things along and keep communication active, and it is very much in their interests to do this as they don't get paid until the property is sold.

WHAT'S NEW?

Over the last ten years there have been substantial changes in buying and selling a property. These range from how you search for a property through to what checks you should make when buying one. Even if you haven't moved for a long time, or even over the last few years, there are likely to be things you will need to do that you didn't have to do last time. Here is a list of the main changes, further details are given in the relevant chapters.

❝ Over the last ten years there have been substantial changes in buying and selling a property. ❞

The internet

This has become a powerful tool for researching the housing market, marketing properties and finding service providers. Relevant websites are provided throughout this book at the appropriate places.

Home Information Packs (HIPs)

From June 2007 it will be mandatory to produce a pack of information about your property before putting it

Chapter 4 (pages 89-122) covers all that you need to know about the process of selling your home, and Chapter 5 (pages 123-54), likewise looks at what you should know about buying a property.

on the market. The seller will, for the first time, be responsible for having the property surveyed, and some of the legal work previously done when an offer was accepted must instead be prepared in advance. This is covered in detail on pages 105–8.

No sale, no fee conveyancing

This change means you don't have to pay the legal fee if your sale falls through. You do, however, still have to pay any charges, such as for searches.

Delays in making offers

People tend to wait to make offers until they have sold/got an offer on their own property. This makes it more likely that their offer will actually be serious and will come to fruition.

Mortgage fees

Mortgage fees, such as administration or booking charges, have increased dramatically.

Proof of identity

You now need to provide the agent (if selling) with proof of identity. You also need to provide your solicitor with the same thing.

Gas and electric checks

These are essential. New laws mean you should have gas and electric checks because when HIPs come in you won't be able to sell your property without the relevant certificates. It is also now illegal for unqualified people to carry out certain electrical work. In the worst case, you may have to rewire a property before you can even put it on the market.

Stamp duty

Stamp duty (now called stamp duty land tax) rate changes are made each year when the government releases its well publicised budget figures, normally in the spring, prior to the new 'government' year: 5 April. As of spring 2006, the current stamp duty rates are: nothing for a property sold at less than £125,000; 1 per cent for £125,001–£250,000; 3 per cent for £250,001–£500,000 and 4 per cent for properties sold at more than £500,001.

The large hike in stamp duty for properties over £250,000 has had an impact on people's ability to find the cash to purchase a property. However, due to the large increase in property prices and the affordability issue for first-time buyers, the nil band has been moved from £60,000 to £120,000.

There are requests for this to be raised further. Increases in stamp duty tend to be made in a rising market and when the government needs some extra cash. While the market appears stable it is likely these rates will remain the same.

Assets, advisers and affordability

This is the reality check: what can you actually, realistically, afford to pay for your new property? This chapter gives advice on how to assess your own finances before entering the mortgage minefield. It takes you through the process of selecting a loan and explains the other, often hidden financial implications of owning property.

How much can you afford?

Before finding your dream home, you need to make sure you can afford to buy and run it. It is surprising just how many people get to the stage of making an offer on a house before realising that they can't actually pay for it.

Sadly, by doing this, they waste their own and, perhaps more importantly, other people's time, too. Worse still, if you take on a mortgage that you can't afford and end up in arrears, you may have a repossession order to cope with and financial trouble for life, so think very hard before you stretch yourself for that 'dream property'. For a full understanding of what you can afford, you first need to have a good grasp of your assets and liabilities.

ASSETS
Your assets are:

Value of your property
If you already own a home that you are selling, calculate the **equity** you will be able to carry over. This is the difference between what you owe on your current mortgage loan (a liability), and what your home is likely to sell for.

> **"** Think very hard before you stretch yourself for that 'dream property'. If you end up in arrears, you may have financial trouble for life. **"**

Get regulated

It is against the law to offer mortgage advice unless you are authorised to do so by the FSA. The information in this book is for guidance only and does not constitute advice, which is best obtained from an independent mortgage adviser or an independent financial adviser (IFA) who specialises in mortgages. Always check that anyone you speak to is regulated by the FSA by going to www.fsa.gov.uk.

 For further analysis of your assets and liabilities, see information on income and expenditure on pages 26-7. The different types of mortgage that are available are covered on pages 36-49 and getting the right mortgage is covered on pages 50-8.

Savings in bank or building society

If you have savings that you can cash, these could allow you to pay a higher deposit on your next property (see page 29), increasing the price you can afford and giving you a wider range of mortgage options.

Shares or other investments

Investment income is not usually included in mortgage calculations because it is not guaranteed. However, if you have any, you could sell some investments to raise the deposit.

- **Make sure** you know the lead time to convert these into cash. Remember that if you are paying a deposit, it needs to be paid at the time of exchange, so you may need to raise extra cash rather than relying on your equity to pay for it.
- **Always consult** an independent financial adviser on the implications of cashing in or using any savings or investments.

LIABILITIES

Your liabilities are:

Mortgage outstanding

This is the amount that is left to be paid on your mortgage. This will depend on the type of mortgage (see pages 42–7) and how long you have had it. Your lender will be able to tell you this figure.

Existing loans

These are any current debts, such as a car loan, hire purchase agreement or a large credit card bill. Such loans may affect your ability to pay a mortgage and therefore the offer that you make.

Cost of moving

There are many costs associated with buying, selling and moving (see pages 30–1) and you will need to include these in your calculations.

❝ If you are taking mortgage advice, always check the adviser is regulated by the FSA. ❞

Assets and liabilities	
Assets	**Liabilities**
• Value of your property • Savings in bank or building society that can be cashed • Shares or other investments that can be cashed	• Mortgage outstanding • Debts, such as loans (car or hire purchase items) • Cost of moving

Assets and liabilities: an example

Assets

Value of your property	£150,000
Savings in bank or building society	£5,000
Shares or other investments	£3,000
Total:	£158,000

Liabilities

Mortgage outstanding	£120,000
Debts, such as loans	£10,000
Cost of moving	£6,000
Total:	£136,000

Net cash available (assets less liabilities): £22,000

In the example calculation given above, the balance between assets and liabilities is £22,000. Some of this could become the deposit you pay on your new property, reducing the amount you need to borrow (see page 29). It can also help give you a financial cushion if you find a property you love and need to accept a lower price on your property.

Changes in your income

You may be due a rise in salary, or if you are paid commission, bonuses or a high proportion of overtime, so you may expect your actual income to go up or down in the near future. It is vital to be realistic about these figures or you may overstretch yourself and risk being unable to afford your mortgage.

INCOME AND EXPENDITURE

Now you know your assets and liabilities, you can make a deeper study of your income and expenditure to help you decide how much mortgage you can afford and how much you will need to run a new property.

Income

Income is the money you earn. Gross income is your earnings before tax and other deductions, after which it is known as net income. Your lender is only likely to count half of income such as overtime, commission or bonuses unless it is guaranteed. You can check (and prove!) your income with your three most recent payslips or the P60 form that is issued each year in April, which gives details of your pay and how much tax has been deducted.

Expenditure

Expenditure is the payments you make, from a chocolate bar paid for with small change to buying a car or the monthly insurance premium. You don't need to be aware of every single purchase, but you do need to know how much you spend each month and what it goes on. Make an honest list of your monthly expenses by checking through your bank and credit card statements. This will tell you how much you're spending on the categories outlined in the table opposite. Keep a note of this figure for later in this chapter. First, though, it is important to be aware of the cost of buying a home.

Monthly expenditure

Use this list as the basis of your calculations for your monthly expenditure. Be honest!

Food and drink £ _____

Clothes £ _____

Household items £ _____

Telephone charges £ _____
- mobile
- landline

TV expenses £ _____
- licence
- digital channels

Fuel £ _____
- oil
- gas
- electricity

School expenses £ _____

Car and travel £ _____
- loan
- fuel
- tax
- servicing
- train/bus/underground

Entertainment £ _____

Holidays £ _____

Subscriptions £ _____

Standing orders and direct debits £ _____

Insurances £ _____
- car
- building
- house contents

Water rates £ _____

Council tax £ _____

Loan and hire purchase repayments £ _____

Other £ _____

COSTS OF BUYING

Buying a property doesn't just mean getting a mortgage and finding somewhere you like. You also need to set money aside for the many costs associated with selling, buying and moving. The chart overleaf outlines the different areas that you need to be aware of when making your plans – legal costs, mortgage fees and removals add up to a surprisingly large amount of money. And then there is the deposit to concern yourself with.

New house, new bills

When looking into the costs of buying, you must also allow for any expenses that would be significantly different in a new home. For example:

- Your new property might be in a higher council tax band, or in a region with higher council tax levels.

- Your commuting costs may be higher.

- Larger houses cost more to run. For example, your utility bills may vary:

1-bedroom flat	£550* per annum
2-bedroom terrace	£600* per annum
3-bedroom semi-detached	£620* per annum
4-bedroom detached	£650* per annum
5-bedroom detached+	£850* per annum

* based on lowest cost utility companies, paying by direct debit for joint gas and electricity

Jargon buster

Arrangement fee A fee charged by some lenders on particular deals

County Court Judgement (CCJ) A judgement for a debt by the county court

Deposit The down payment on a property, paid when contracts are exchanged

Equity The difference between the price of a property sold and the loan on it

Exchange of contracts A binding legal agreement that confirms the intention to transfer ownership of a property between a buyer and seller

Higher lending charge premium The payment that needs to be made for a higher lending charge (see page 48 for more information)

Survey A report on the condition of a property

The deposit

The deposit is the cash down payment you make on your new home. The higher your deposit, the better interest rates you are likely to have access to on your mortgage, so it is worth considering paying as much as you can afford. When you have a large deposit (more than 10 per cent), you'll also avoid the possibility of a higher lending charge. These charges can be several hundreds of pounds or even £2,000–£3,000, depending on the price of the property.

Very few mortgage companies will be prepared to offer you a loan of 100 per cent of the value of the home. Those that do are likely to charge a higher interest rate. This is because you present a higher risk to them than someone who has put their own money down as deposit (see also the advice on higher lending charges on page 48).

Most lenders will offer up to 95 per cent of the value that their own valuer puts on the property, but this is not always the case. For example, some mortgage lenders don't lend on timber or thatched properties. So be aware that it is not just your ability to make a certain level of mortgage payments that determines your mortgage offer, it also depends on the type and age of a property, its condition and other factors, which are discussed on pages 61 and 146–50.

The low-down on deposits

Buyers are usually expected by the vendor and their legal company to pay a 5 per cent deposit on properties under £99,999 at time of exchange (which means a £90,000 house requires a £4,500 deposit) and 10 per cent for those costing more than this (so on a £200,000 home it would be £20,000), although this can vary. The amount of deposit you pay is subject to an agreement between the buyer and seller via the solicitor. The higher the deposit versus the value of the property, the more access you will have to competitive mortgage deals.

Thanks, mum and dad

An increasing social trend is for parents or grandparents to gift or loan money to their offspring so that they can buy their first home. On average they lend or give £17,000 if they can afford it – and some relatives even take on a loan themselves to achieve this.

 There are a few websites with budget planners to help you with your calculations: www.abbey.com; www.designsonproperty.co.uk; www.easier2move.co.uk and www.switchwithwhich.co.uk/mortgage.

Costs of buying and moving home

Use this table to give you an approximate idea of the costs of buying and moving home. Select the relevant figures for legal, mortgage and removals costs and then add together for the total cost. If you are selling, take the value of your property and multiply it by 1.8 per cent to gain an idea of the fee you are likely to have to pay to an estate agent.

	Value of property				
	Up to £99k	£100–£249k	£250–400k	£401–£500k	£501+
Legal costs					
Fees	465	560	590	650	700
Searches	175	200	225	250	250
Stamp duty	0	see ready reckoner		see ready reckoner	
Money transfer	35	35	35	35	35
Land Registry fee	200	200	250	250	420
Leasehold◆	115	115	115	115	115
Sub-total					

	Value of property				
	Up to £99k	£100–£249k	£250–400k	£401–£500k	£501+
Mortgage fees					
Valuation	175	265	420	420	420
Arrangement fee▲	300	300	300	300	300
And/or booking fee	250	250	250	250	250
Higher lending charge● For guidance, see www.switchwithwhich.co.uk/mortgage/beware/hlcs.html					
Survey fee■					
– Either homebuyer	300	300	550	650	800
– Or building	500	500	700	800	1200
Sub-total					

	Value of property				
	Up to £99k	£100–£249k	£250–400k	£401–£500k	£501+
Removals					
Hire a van	125	125	Not Recommended	Not Recommended	Not Recommended
Removal company	450	600	800	1000	1500
Add packing by removal company	100	150	200	250	300
Sub-total					
Total					

* Only add this figure if you are buying a flat.
▲ If you are obtaining a mortgage, check whether you need to pay an arrangement and/or booking fee (see page 51).
■ A higher lending charge is only appropriate in certain cases – see the Which? website shown on the table and also page 48.
■ The choice of survey is yours to make – for information, see pages 152–3.

Stamp duty land tax ready reckoner

As of spring 2006, the current stamp duty rates are:

Property value	Stamp duty
Up to £125,000	Nil
£125,001–£250,000	1%
£250,001–£500,000	3%
More than £500,001	4%

Other factors

Other things that can affect how much lenders will offer you, and therefore how much you can afford, include:

Credit worthiness

Anyone who lends you money will assess your credit worthiness. Lenders do this by checking your credit file. This is a record of your financial history together with other information, such as details of any bankruptcies and **County Court Judgements** (CCJs). Lenders will assess this information together with the details you provided on your application form and any information they already hold on you. Lenders use different methods of assessing you, so you may be rejected by one and accepted by another.

If you find you're refused credit by mainstream lenders, there are specialist lenders who may lend to you even though your credit history means you're a greater risk.

If you think any of the information on your credit file may be wrong, you can request a copy of your file. There are three main credit reference agencies (CRAs): Equifax, Experian and Callcredit (see below). If you send them a cheque or pay £2 online, they will send you a copy of your file.

If there is a mistake on your file:

- **Write to the CRA** and ask it to remove or change the entry explaining why it's wrong and sending any evidence.
- **The CRA has 28 days** to act. In the meantime, the entry is marked as disputed on your file.
- **If the CRA decides** not to make a correction, you can send it a notice of correction to be added to your file. This should explain why you think the entry is wrong and point out any mitigating circumstances.

> **❝Anyone who lends you money will assess your credit worthiness.❞**

Being self-employed

You will need to provide evidence of income for the last two or three years depending on the lender because the mortgage company will treat the average profit that you pay tax on for that period as your income. If you haven't been self-employed that long, you may have less choice of mortgages and be asked to pay a

 If you think there may be incorrect information on your credit file, contact the three main credit checking companies. Go to websites www.equifax.co.uk (Equifax), www.experian. co.uk (Experian) or www.callcredit.plc.uk.

higher deposit or higher interest rate. Alternatively, you can apply for a self-certification mortgage (see page 46).

Not having a permanent job

If, for example, you are a contract worker, you may be asked to get a letter from your employer confirming they will continue to give you work, or to provide other evidence that your earnings will continue to be the same.

If you have ever been declared bankrupt

Buyers with these circumstances tend to be offered more expensive (i.e. higher rate) mortgages as the loan companies limit their risks. Contact an independent financial adviser for help.

| Joint mortgages |

Unmarried couples are usually treated the same as a husband and wife in working out how much they can borrow. Gay or lesbian couples can also apply, as well as groups of two or more friends who are combining their finances to get on the property ladder (they are known as multiple applicants, see pages 140-1). However, it may be harder for them to find a lender willing to take on the loan because if one mortgage owner moves out, the remaining person may still be responsible for all of the loan.

HOW MUCH CAN I BORROW?

The key concept here is affordability. There can be a big difference between what some lenders are prepared to offer and what you should realistically take on. This is because interest rates and costs can go up as well as down. It pays to have a good grasp of your own finances, giving you a realistic view of what you can afford to pay out each month, even if things change for the worse. The table overleaf gives two examples of annual income and expenditure. The figures used are for guidance only, because the affordability factor will be different for everybody. Base your own calculations on the monthly expenditure table you drew up from the list on page 27.

The maximum amount you can borrow is calculated from your net income, which means your regular salary. Your lender is only likely to count half of income such as overtime, commission or bonuses unless it is guaranteed. However, they may look more favourably on an applicant with good future prospects

❝ There is a big difference between what some lenders are prepared to offer and what you should realistically take on – interest rates and costs can go up as well as down. ❞

Example of annual income versus expenditure

Base your deductions on the figures from your monthly expenditure calculations (see page 27), multiplying them by 12.

	Working couple with company car and no children	Working couple with two children
Income		
Salary 1	£20,000	£20,000
Salary 2	£10,000	£10,000
Total income	£30,000	£30,000
Annual income after tax	£21,000	£21,000
Deductions		
Food and drink	£3,640	£6,240
Clothes	£800	£1,000
Household expenses♦	£1,440	£1,600
School expenses	None	£750
Car loan	None	£2,000
Fuel	None	£1,200
Entertainment/holidays	£5,000	£1,500
Subscriptions	£150	None
Standing orders and direct debits▲	£100	£50
Insurances	£300	None
Water rates	£500	£500
Council tax	£1,200	£1,000
Loan and hire purchase repayments	None	£600
Total deductions	£13,130	£16,440
Income minus deductions	£7,870	£4,560

♦ These include costs of fuel and running a telephone and television

▲ Do not include any current mortgage payments you are making in this figure

The final figure in each column shows the amount that each couple have available each year to cover a mortgage and the higher costs of running a larger home. Clearly the first couple can afford much more than the second couple, even though their income is identical. This illustrates the importance of considering what you can afford rather than just working from multiples of income.

of a secure, high income, such as doctors, accountants and solicitors.

How much can I afford?

This is the crucial question. Bear in mind that if you are planning to start or increase the size of your family, your income will be affected. During the advice process, your broker or adviser can ask you if this is the case as it will certainly influence your ability to make the monthly payments. It is important during this advice process to divulge as much information as possible to make sure you gain the best recommendation for your circumstances.

Income would also be reduced by either partner suffering long-term illness, taking a career break or re-training. Remember also that UK interest rates have stayed low for several years and we have become used to this, but if they rise, monthly payments can go up substantially. The message is: don't mortgage yourself to the maximum, because there is no safety margin if things go wrong, and that could eventually cost you your home.

WHAT CAN GO WRONG WITH FINANCING A MOVE?

Paying a mortgage is a big responsibility and there are times when circumstances will affect your ability to continue paying it.

Interest rates going up

This can have a dramatic impact on your monthly payments – for more information, see page 36.

Valuation lower than price

Sometimes the lender's surveyor values a property at a lower figure than the agreed selling price. This could be because they have a different perspective on the local market or because they find faults with the property. You could decide to use this information to re-negotiate the price, or you might decide from your own soundings and research that you are willing to stick to the agreed price. The difference need not be a problem if you can make it up and the lender is still happy to loan you the sum you need. It may, however, influence their willingness to loan 100 per cent or 95 per cent of the value.

Losing a job or income

Any change in your financial status, from losing a job or contract to getting less commission or bonus will affect how much you can afford. You will need to discuss this with your loan provider and decide for yourself if you still want to go ahead with the move.

 There are various schemes designed to help someone who can no longer afford to pay a mortgage. Ranging from short-term measures to something more drastic, these are all covered in detail on pages 61-3.

Choosing a mortgage

Getting a mortgage is one of the biggest financial transactions of your life, with implications on your financial well-being for decades. If you get it wrong and don't keep checking if you are on the best deal, it could cost you tens of thousands of pounds.

There are more than 140 mortgage providers, many of whom offer a wide range of products. Finding the right one for you is tricky and takes some work, but it is well worth doing this before looking at properties because you will be in a better position to put in an offer that you know you can afford. You will be able to negotiate knowing what finances you have available.

RISK VERSUS REWARD

Lenders will typically be glad to lend you as much as they can – subject to each lender's criteria – because in that way they make more money out of you. However, it's all about risk and reward. The more you borrow, the higher the chance you might not be able to repay your mortgage at some stage.

As a borrower, the most important consideration is the effect that different interest rates would have on your monthly payments (see table, right). Interest rates are predicted to stay around the current historically low rates. However, consider what would happen if there was an economic crisis

Mortgage definition

A mortgage is a loan secured on a property. This means that the mortgage company owns all or part of your home until you pay back the money. You can't sell it without paying off the loan, and if you do not keep up the agreed monthly payments, the lender can take possession of the home.

How repayments can vary

This table shows how monthly repayments on a £100,000 repayment mortgage over 25 years would vary with a changing interest rate.

Interest rate payment	Monthly
5%	£591.27
6%	£651.88
7%	£715.08
8%	£780.65
9%	£848.38
10%	£918.06
11%	£989.50
12%	£1,062.49

as this could cause interest rates to rise to 10 or even 15 per cent (as we saw in the early 1990s). A good discipline is to check the highest interest rate payments you could afford to pay to stay in the property by using some of the online mortgage calculators given in the box at the foot of page 29. If it suits you, you could look at a fixed or capped interest rate to help avoid this problem (see also page 44).

On top of this, don't rely on property values always increasing, and consider what would happen if you had to sell within one or two years.

WHERE TO GO FOR A MORTGAGE

First, work out how much you can afford (see page 33). Get proof of your income(s), such as wage slips for the last six months or a P60 form, or a letter from your employer confirming your salary and any bonuses or commission that form part of your income and any other relevant financial information, such as life insurance or critical illness policies. Some of these may be provided by your employer.

It is well worth shopping around for your mortgage. Start by investigating online, because you can quickly change figures to see how they affect the monthly payments. Seek advice from your current lender and a mortgage broker or an independent financial adviser as you are then less likely to make an expensive mistake. There are several sources for this information.

> **❝ Find the right mortgage provider and you can negotiate knowing what finances you have available. ❞**

Websites

Which? (www.switchwithwhich.co.uk) and the Financial Services Authority (www.fsa.gov.uk) both have websites containing independent information about mortgages. They also both offer a mortgage search that lets you search for mortgages with particular features. The Which? sites let you compare different mortgages based on the total cost of the mortgage.

Lenders

Lenders, such as banks and building societies, can usually recommend mortgages from their own range only. If you've already got an existing mortgage, it's worth approaching your

---

 For information on finding a competitive mortgage, see the following websites: www.switchwithwhich.co.uk, www.moneynet.co.uk and also www.moneysupermarket.co.uk.

lender to see what deal they'll offer you. It's always worth trying to negotiate although some lenders offer better deals to new customers than to existing ones.

Intermediaries

Instead of going direct to a lender you can go to an intermediary, such as a mortgage broker or independent financial adviser, to help you find a mortgage. They may search the whole market or they may only be able to offer mortgages from a selection of lenders. Some have their own deals that they have negotiated with lenders and which aren't available elsewhere. They must tell you at the outset how many lenders they are searching against.

They must also explain whether they will charge you a fee for their service or whether they'll rely on the comission from the lender for their

income. If they take the commission option, then you won't pay anything for the service you receive. Any fee charged is usually a percentage of the

" Mortgage brokers charge for their time either through a commission fee or as a percentage of the mortgage. Agree in advance which option you will use. "

A mortgage broker can only use the term 'independent' if they search the whole market for a mortgage and offer you the option to pay a fee for their advice.

For more information on choosing a mortgage lender or intermediary, see pages 50-5, which describes the different levels of service and explains how you can assess what's best for you.

Your rights

In October 2004, the Financial Services Authority (FSA) took over the regulation of most mortgage sales, replacing the previous system, which was known as the Mortgage Code. Anyone involved in mortgage lending, administration, advice and arranging must be a member of the FSA by law. The FSA's **Mortgage Conduct of Business** states that mortgage lenders and intermediaries must:

Give clear information

This relates to mortgages and morgage services and the information must be given in a standard 'keyfacts' format so that it is easy to compare mortgages and services from different lenders.

Make price information obvious

All price information should appear in advertising and marketing material, including the annual percentage rate (APR), but it must be clearly laid out.

Recommend a suitable mortgage

The advice that is given must be based on your personal needs and circumstances.

Offer greater protection

Should you get into arrears with your mortgage, there are rules in place about the steps firms should take to treat you fairly.

Offer redress

If you have a dispute with your lender, you can take your complaint to the Financial Ombudsman Service. The Financial Services compensation scheme, which can pay compensation if a firm is unable to unlikely to be able to pay is also available to you.

mortgage, such as 0.2 per cent or sometimes as high as 1 per cent. If you choose to use an independent financial adviser, check that they specialise in mortgages as some don't.

Insurance companies

Life insurance companies employ salespeople who are also mortgage brokers. Like independent financial advisers, they may or may not specialise in mortgages.

Estate agents

Some estate agents employ people in their branches who can offer mortgage advice. These will either be mortgage brokers, independent financial adviers or life insurance representatives.

Employers such as banks and financial institutions

Sometimes companies offer competitive mortgages as a fringe benefit to their employees. Other large employers may have links to financial companies, which give preferential rates to employees. Check if these offers are available to you and what the position would be if you were to leave.

Builders or developers

Builders or developers can arrange loans as an incentive to buy their properties, often in a part-exchange deal where they sell your current home. This may be convenient but

check that their offer stands up against others on the market and if there are any restrictions on their lending, such as high penalty clauses.

GETTING A MAP

A Mortgage Agreement in Principle (MAP) is an expression of a mortgage lender's willingness to enter into an agreement subject to other conditions being met, such as full credit checks and a satisfactory property valuation. Obtaining a MAP through a lender shows you are serious about buying a property and have the finances available that you claim. This could be invaluable if you are competing with someone else for a property you both like: the seller is more likely to opt for someone who can prove their ability to afford the property. It also saves you any embarrassment of having to pull out from a deal having made an offer that you later found was more than you can afford.

A Mortgage Agreement in Principle costs nothing and are usually valid for three months. They involve checks on your credit rating, earnings and affordability. You can obtain one online from many mortgage lenders in about 15 minutes, or get one from a branch of a bank or building society or an independent financial adviser, mortgage broker or other intermediary – something well worth doing if you are serious about buying property.

HOW LONG?

You can take out a mortgage covering any period – usually up to your retirement age as a maximum – but the standard term is 25 years. The longer the mortgage term, the less your monthly payments, but the more you will eventually pay in interest. As a result, the faster you can pay off your mortgage loan, the less interest you will pay. So in summary, taking a £40,000 loan for 15 rather than 25 years would cost more each month, but could save about £20,000 in interest over the term of the loan (see the chart, below). Some key questions will help you choose:

When do you want to pay off the loan?

This will help you decide whether you are happy with the standard 25-year loan, to increase it to 30 years or reduce it to ten years, depending on what you can afford each month and when you want to be mortgage free.

The costs of a repayment mortgage over different terms

This graph shows the costs of a £100,000 repayment mortgage with an interest rate of 5 per cent over five years. It demonstrates the benefits of choosing a shorter term if you can afford it. Although a shorter term means higher monthly repayments, this has the same effect as overpaying your mortgage – more of your money goes towards paying off your mortgage and less in interest.

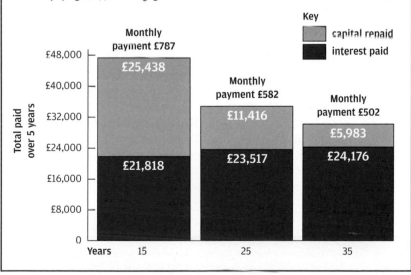

Will you want to pay off lump sums or overpay at any stage?

The faster you pay off your mortgage, the less interest charges you pay. So if you plan to pay off your mortgage with any spare earnings or money you receive, make sure that you choose a rate and lender that will allow you to do this without any penalties. Some, for example, won't let you pay extra while you are on a special interest rate deal (such as a fixed rate). Others may limit the amount you can repay. For example, some allow you to overpay by 10 per cent of the loan value per annum. For example, if you owe £100,000 in year one, you can overpay by a maximum of £10,000, then if it drops to £85,000 in the next year, £8,500 and so on (see also page 47). Paying off your mortgage early can save you tens of thousands of pounds in interest rate payments.

TYPES OF MORTGAGE

It can be very confusing picking your way through the mortgage minefield, and it is certainly worth getting as much advice as you can. Everyone's finances are different and people have varying attitudes to risk, which will influence their choice of mortgage. If you already have a mortgage, moving

❝The choice of repayment versus interest-only mortgage relates to how you repay your mortgage. ❞

house is a natural time to review it, re-assessing not just the amount of your loan, but whether it is the best deal available for your current circumstances. This may have changed since your current mortgage was arranged.

Starting with the basics, there are two key types of mortgage: repayment and interest only. These choices are only about how you repay your mortgage. The interest rates (there are more choices here, see pages 43–4) determine how much you pay and whether your payment will vary. It is really important to gain independent financial advice on the best way to repay your mortgage for your circumstances (see page 35).

Repayment mortgage

This means that you are paying off both the loan and the interest owed in monthly instalments. So at the end of a typical loan period of 25 years, the

For more information on dealing with mortgage lenders and intermediaries, see pages 50–1 where matters such as the different level of service and initial disclosure documents are explained.

whole sum has been paid off and you own the property outright. Monthly payments are always higher than for interest-only loans. A repayment mortgage is the only type that guarantees you'll repay the mortgage by the end of your chosen term.

Interest-only mortgage

This involves paying only the interest on the loan, so after a typical loan period of 25 years, you still owe the mortgage lender the original amount you borrowed. You have to re-pay the loan amount and most borrowers pay separately into a savings or investment acount to ensure they have the capital to do so. Typical investments used include an ISA or pension schemes. The aim is for them to provide you with enough to pay off the balance of the loan when the term ends. Some investment plans have not performed as well as expected in recent years, and you may be left with a shortfall, still owing the lender money. On the other hand, if the policy does well, you may have enough money to pay back the lender

" The longer the mortgage term, the less your monthly payments, but the more you will eventually pay in interest. "

and have additional cash to spend too. It is your responsibility to ensure you have enough to repay the loan at the end of the mortgage.

TYPES OF INTEREST RATE

There are five different ways in which your interest can be applied to a mortgage.

Standard variable rate (SVR)

This is the standard product offered by lenders and is broadly linked to the Bank of England base rate, plus a margin (lender's profit!). However, the level of the SVR very much depends on the lender and there is a wide range on the market. There is also no guarantee that the SVR will move in line with the bank base rate.

Fixed rate

This means the interest rate stays the same for a set time (usually two to five years), whatever happens to the base rate, which is set by the Bank of England. At the end of that period, the rate typically reverts to the lender's standard variable rate. In reality, you can then re-negotiate the loan or even consider switching to another lender to get a better deal. If the variable rate falls below what you are paying during the set period, you can lose out. If it rises above your fixed rate during this period, then this type of rate works in your favour.

The main advantage of this arrangement is that you know what your monthly repayments will be for a certain number of years, allowing you to plan the rest of your finances with some security.

Capped rate

This type of deal guarantees the maximum rate you will pay for a set period (generally three to five years). If the base rate falls, so does your rate and the amount you pay. You tend to pay more for a capped rate than a fixed rate. If the rate rises, it only rises as far as the 'capped' rate. Capped rate mortgages are attractive when it is uncertain whether interest rates are likely to rise or fall. Be aware, too, · that some deals have a 'collar rate', which limits how low the rate can drop, potentially reducing your benefit if the base rate falls significantly.

Discounted rate

This is a set reduction from the standard variable rate for a set period of two to five years. So if your reduction is 2 per cent and the rate is 6 per cent, you'll pay 4 per cent – and if the lender's rate rises to 7 per cent your rate will rise from 4 to 5 per cent, causing your monthly payments to rise too. This appeals to customers attracted by a lower rate than a fixed or capped rate and who are prepared for payments to vary. It is an attractive option when interest rates are on a downward path as the lender will have to pass on any discounts to you. Remember, though, that the lender isn't obliged to lower its standard variable rate when the base rate falls and although they generally do, it isn't necessarily straightaway and does not always move by the same number of percentage points.

Base rate tracker

A base rate tracker is similar to a discounted rate, but it ties your rate above or below the Bank of England base rate. So if you are on a 0.5 per cent discounted deal and the base rate is 4 per cent, you pay 3.5 per cent. Changes in the base rate affect your monthly payments – and you gain the full advantage of the drop if they fall, but similarly your rate rises with the base rate if it rises. Trackers ensure you will benefit fully if rates fall.

❝ The bank base rate is set by the Bank of England – it can go up as well as down and will have a bearing on your mortgage repayments. ❞

 Remember that each of these different types of interest rate – and the other incentives listed on pages 45-6 – can apply to both repayment and interest-only mortgages, which were described on page 42.

Combination deals

These are deals with several of the elements just described. For example, you might get a one-year fixed rate, which then turns into a two-year discount rate.

OTHER INCENTIVES

There are other types of deals that are marketed by mortgage lenders to try to gain your business and these can be given with any of their mortgages and interest rate deals. Before you take up any of these deals, check that it is right for you, not just in the short-term as it may cost you more money in the long run.

Cash back

This is an incentive to sign up with a lender where you get some of the loan (say 5 per cent) back in cash. This can help cover the costs of a new car or furnishing a new home when you are buying a new home, but you are likely to be tied into the lender for a period of time and may pay a higher interest rate than on other deals.

Flexible or offset mortgages

Flexible and offset mortgages offer non-standard features, which can be useful to some people in certain circumstances, although they charge a higher interest rate as a result.

A flexible mortgage allows you to increase your monthly payments and pay lump sums off your mortgage. These overpayments reduce your

 Some low interest rate or cash back deals can be more expensive than they might appear because you are tied to a lender's uncompetitive rate for years, or you may be forced to take out their home insurance or payment protection policies. Beware of picking a deal that looks great in the short-term, without looking at the whole cost of the loan over the period. Be aware, too, of lenders that impose early repayment charges if you switch to another provider or make early repayments.

mortgage balance so you end up paying less interest in the long run. Some deals also allow you to borrow back any overpayments you have made, take a payment holiday or make underpayments.

If you think you're only interested in making overpayments, consider a standard mortgage instead as these tend to be cheaper and some allow overpayments. But check carefully that there aren't any restrictions on the amount you can overpay.

Flexible mortgages can also allow a 'draw down' facility allowing you to borrow more money. For example, you might buy a property that needs some work. You think you've budgeted well for the work but you find it goes over and you need more money, often quickly! One way of doing this is to borrow more than you need and 'draw down' the additional money if required. For example, you may need a £140,000 mortgage for the property and intend to spend £20,000 of that sum renovating. This figure then increases to £30,000 due to costs not anticipated and changes you make in the specification. If you had taken out a £150,000 mortgage with a £10,000 'draw down' facility, then you would be able to cover the increase in costs. But if you don't

> **"A flexible mortgage can be particularly complex and require careful monitoring, so always get independent mortgage advice before taking one on. "**

need it, you don't draw it down and hence don't pay for it. Bear in mind that the extra amount you borrow will be secured on your house along with the rest of the loan. And if you choose to spread the repayments over the usual mortgage term (25 years, say), you'll end up paying more back than if you went for a shorter term unsecured personal loan.

An offset mortgage combines your savings, and in some cases your current account, with your mortgage. In effect, your savings or account balance reduces the amount of the loan and hence cuts the interest paid on it. You can still take out your money from your savings or current account, but you will then have to pay more interest as your loan will have increased.

For example, if you have a £100,000 mortgage and have amassed savings of £10,000, you can pay this sum into a linked savings account, effectively reducing your mortgage to £90,000. So you'll pay less interest as your loan has shrunk – but you won't earn interest on your savings. The theory is that if your savings earn a lower rate of interest than what you are paying on your mortgage, you are better off using your savings to reduce your mortgage. The more money you have available to offset against the mortgage, the lower your payments will be. The arrangement is of most benefit to higher-rate tax payers with substantial savings (more than 15 per cent of the value of the mortgage).

These are complex arrangements requiring careful monitoring, so it is vital to get independent mortgage advice before taking on this or any type of mortgage.

Self-certification mortgage

If you are self-employed, it can be difficult to prove your income and it may vary dramatically throughout the year or from one month to the next. Most lenders contact your accountant or employer, verifying your status, but not your income. New businesses or those whose accountant has minimised the declared income and are unable to provide the information required can opt for a self-certification mortgage. This involves a declaration of income without proof. However, this is not a licence to get any level of mortgage you want. The lender will carry out credit checks or ask for information from your bank, accountant or other source, such as a commercial landlord. Lenders tend to charge a higher interest rate and limit the loan to 75 per cent or 90 per cent of the property value. As a result, you have to find a much higher than average deposit to buy the property.

BRIDGING LOANS

If you have an offer accepted on a property but can't sell yours or are suddenly faced with a delay in selling your own – perhaps due to the death or unexpected withdrawal of your buyer – you may consider a bridging loan. This is a new loan while you still have your old mortgage, and it is expensive: there is usually a setting-up fee of 0.5–1.5 per cent, and the interest rate is generally 2–2.5 per cent above base rate. There are two kinds of bridging loan that you can consider:

- **Closed,** when you have exchanged on your purchase and need cover for a set period until the selling contract is exchanged.
- **Open,** if you have not sold your property. There is no time limit so the costs could be very high.

If you are in this position, you might be better off renting out your old home instead. This will allow you to move to your new property, make at least a contribution to your existing mortgage, and remove the pressure to sell fast. You would need to convert your mortgage to a **buy-to-let** arrangement.

HIDDEN COSTS

Rather like a restaurant bill where a cover charge, extra drinks, a phantom dessert and a service charge (with an extra box for 'gratuities') appear at the end to inflate the cost, mortgages can soak up more of your money than you expected. Some expensive 'extras' to watch out for include the following.

Early repayment charges

Early repayment charges (also known as redemption penalties) can apply when you repay the mortgage in full or in part. Some lenders don't charge this if you remain owing as little as £1, whereas others will charge if you pay off any amount at all, so it is important to be aware of the small print before you confirm your move.

Jargon buster

Key facts about our mortgage services An illustration showing the mortgage costs, features and terms and conditions. You should be given this for a mortgage that is recommended to you if you take advice, or one for each of the mortgages you are interested in if you don't take advice (see also page 56) and any new lending agreement.

When moving house, you effectively pay off the existing loan and take out a new one. You may, however, be charged several months' worth of mortgage payments as a penalty for redeeming earlier than stated in the agreement, unless your loan is classed as '**portable**', in which case your mortgage arrangement can be transferred to the new property.

Arrangement fee

Many lenders charge an 'arrangement fee' for 'reserving funds' for special deals like fixed-rate mortgages and discounted rate mortgages. These can be a weighty expense of around £400 or in some cases more. Other lenders are charging anything up to 1.5 per cent of the mortgage, which can be in the thousands. Some lenders then suggest that you 'add' this to the mortgage, but this will cost you more in interest charges over the term of your mortgage.

Higher lending charge

This is a charge you may have to pay if you have a deposit of less than 10 per cent. The fee pays for insurance that protects the lender if you default on payments and they have to sell the property at a loss. It doesn't protect you in any way.

Advisers' fees

No one works for nothing, and certainly not financial advisers and mortgage brokers, who will charge a fee for advice or take commission from the lender they recommend if you sign up with them (see page 38). Fees can be up to 1.5 per cent of your loan, or around £75 per hour. Check this out with the mortgage broker or independent financial adviser before you commit. At the start of the meeting, the adviser should explain what level of service he or she can offer, how the adviser will be paid for it, how many lenders they search against and who regulates his or her activities (for more information, see page 50).

However, these fees can be offset by any beneficial terms the adviser negotiates on your behalf. You have a right to know what commission fee or other payment (which is declared on a document entitled **key facts about our mortgage services** – see page 56) will be made to them, and can then judge for yourself if you think this is reasonable. After all, you are the one funding it.

Banking services

Your deposit and mortgage money will be transferred electronically, for which you will be charged. Fees vary from £20 to £50 and it is worth asking what they are and whether transfers can be made at the same time to avoid multiple charges.

OTHER FINANCIAL PRODUCTS TO CONSIDER

Buying a property with a mortgage is a major financial commitment that you may choose to protect with various insurance policies. Your lender may recommend some and might also insist that you have life insurance. Which policies you eventually decide to take out will depend on your personal circumstances, your attitude to risk and any independent advice you receive.

Life insurance

This means that if you die, a lump sum equivalent to the sum insured will be paid, which should be set to the value of the mortgage – or the part of the mortgage that you are responsible for. Level term assurance runs for a set period, usually the mortgage term, and is suitable if you have an interest-only mortgage as the sum assured stays the same throughout the term of the insurance. If you have a repayment mortgage, you are more likely to be advised to go for a decreasing term assurance (also known as mortgage protection cover) which guarantees to pay a reduced sum each year, matching the remaining debt left on the loan. It tends to have lower premiums than level term assurance because the benefit reduces with time. You should check from time to time that your cover is sufficient to cover your outstanding debt.

Critical illness cover (CIC)

This pays the sum insured, which should be set to the value of the mortgage (or the part that you are

responsible for) if you suffer a severe illness as defined in their terms and conditions. The premiums will depend on your age and general health as well as the amount of the loan. The policy will only cover certain specified illnesses, such as a heart attack, stroke or a terminal illness – not more common problems such as back trouble or stress. Do check what is and is not included before paying out for this type of cover.

Income protection insurance or permanent health insurance (PHI)

PHI pays you a regular income if you suffer from a long-term illness, which is designed to replace any loss of income from employment. Again, the premiums will depend on the same factors as critical illness cover. If you are in a full-time job, you may have this cover already – check with your employer.

Accident, sickness and unemployment cover

This pays out a regular income if you have an accident, are made redundant or suffer some forms of sickness. It only covers mortgage payments and is often limited to the first 12 or 24 months.

Getting the best mortgage

When you move house, you will have to reassess your mortgage:
you will either have to redeem your existing mortgage or take your
current one to your new property. Either way, it makes sense at this
juncture to go a step further and check whether your deal is the best
on the market.

Surprisingly, only half of us change lender when we move home. Lots of people also stick with their lender for buildings and contents insurance, mortgage protection and life cover, which is convenient but can be expensive versus other companies. It always pays to shop around.

Start by familiarising yourself with the types of mortgages on offer (as explained in this book on pages 42–4 and at www.switchwithwitch. co.uk. Start by talking to your existing lender if you have one to see what they can offer. Also consult a mortgage broker or independent financial adviser or someone else that you trust or has previously helped a friend or relative, and then compare and query the advice.

> **❝ It pays to shop around for a mortgage but take plenty of advice, too, such as from a mortgage broker or IFA. ❞**

MORTGAGE LENDERS AND INTERMEDIARIES

Under mortgage regulations, lenders and intermediaries must either be authorised by the Financial Services Authority (FSA) or be an appointed representative of an authorised firm. Lenders and intermediaries offer two levels of service that you will be asked to choose from.

- **Advised service:** you'll receive a recommendation on which of the mortgages that they can provide is most suitable for you. If the mortgage turns out to be the wrong one for you, you can complain to the firm and you claim compensation for any loss. Unless you are very confident about choosing a mortgage yourself, it makes sense to opt for the advised service.
- **Non-advised service:** you'll receive information only and will be responsible for making your own choice. The lender will ask you pre-scripted questions to narrow down the mortgages on which they give

you information. This level of service offers you no protection.

Initial disclosure document (IDD)

When you first contact a firm, you should be given a document entitled 'Key facts about our mortgage services' (this is also known as an initial disclosure document). It will set out whether the adviser is going to give you advice and a recommendation or just information, whether you will pay a fee for the service and whose mortgages it offers. For example, lenders, such as banks and building societies, can usually only recommend mortgages from their own range, whereas a broker may search the whole market or be linked to a selection of lenders.

The cost of advice

Mortgage brokers make their money in fees from you, sometimes as high as 1 per cent of the mortgage – so on a £100,000 loan, you would pay £1,500 just for the advice or they take commission from the lender.

IFAs will either charge by the hour (usually around £75 plus VAT, and it is about a day's work to sort out the deal), or gain a commission from the lender (a 'procurement fee'). IFAs will often deduct their commission from a final fee if they are charging by the hour.

> **❝** Always read the IDD and ask questions about anything you don't understand. **❞**

CHOOSING THE RIGHT MORTGAGE

To make the choice that is right for you, you need to ask the right questions and be sure that you understand the answers (see overleaf and pages 54–5). A good financial adviser, whether an independent person or a representative of a lender, should be able to explain the pros and cons of your various options and justify the advice that is given. If the adviser proves unable to do this to your satisfaction, you should take your custom elsewhere.

An adviser should start discussions with you with a financial audit similar in approach to that on pages 24–35. They will also ask you about your attitude to risk as this has a bearing on the product they will suggest.

 To find an independent financial adviser, go to www.fsa.gov.uk, www.impartial.co.uk and www.find.co.uk. Always check on www.fsa.gov.uk/register to see if your adviser is authorised to offer advice.

Key questions: which adviser?

Here is a checklist of key questions that will help you make your decision as to which adviser to give your mortgage business to. Your adviser should give you all this information when you contact them as a document entitled 'Key facts about our mortgage services'.

" Are you authorised to give mortgage advice? "

Advisers must either be directly authorised as an individual by the FSA or represent an FSA authorised firm. You can check if they are covered by the regulations on www.fsa.gov.uk/pages/register. They should also have passed the Certificate in Mortgage Advice and Practice (CMAP) or Financial Planning Certificate (FPC) exams.

" How much of the mortgage market do you have access to? "

Lenders usually only offer mortgages from their own mortgage range. Some IFAs and mortgage brokers only offer mortgages from their preferred lenders, which could restrict the choice of products they make available to you.

" What level of service do you provide? "

They may make a recommendation after they have assessed your needs or provide information only and leave you to choose which mortgage to go for. Only if you buy with advice can you complain to the firm and expect compensation if the mortgage turns out to be unsuitable.

" How will you charge me for advice? "

Intermediaries will either charge you a fee or be paid commission by the lender. They must tell you which of these applies and how much they expect to earn from your transaction. In effect, you are paying for their time and expertise (see page 51).

Key questions: which mortgage?

Make sure your adviser covers the following points to ensure you get as much information about the mortgages on offer as possible. Much of this information should be covered in the key facts illustration your adviser will give you.

"What types of mortgage are available, what are their advantages and disadvantages and how would they suit me?"

The advice should include references to the types of mortgage referred to on page 42.

"What different ways can I repay my mortgage and what are their pros and cons?"

You should be told about repayment and interest-only mortgages including the various ways of repaying the loan sum for the latter.

"What are the risks?"

Your adviser should explain the difference in risk between repayment and interest-only mortgages. You should also be told about the risks of variable rate mortgages and the risk of your income falling.

"What is the interest rate and how does it compare with the Bank of England base rate?"

The adviser should explain what the rate is, how long it applies for and if it is variable or fixed. If there is an initial rate, the adviser should also tell you what it will change to and when.

"Can I afford this mortgage?"

If you're getting advice, your adviser has a duty to take reasonable steps to ensure you can afford the mortgage he or she recommends. Even if you don't get advice, the adviser should check that you can afford the repayments now and in the future.

"How much are the monthly payments? What would they be if the variable rate rises by 1, 3 or 5 percentage points?"

This information will help you decide if you are able to face the risk of higher payments. You should also be told the effect of any change of rate after the initial period.

"How much will I pay in total, including any fees?"

To compare mortgages, you need to know the full cost, including any fees you'll pay. Check whether you would have to pay any of the fees if the house purchase falls through. If fees are added to the mortgage, rather than paying them upfront, you will pay interest on them for the whole term, so check out how much you would be paying in interest on these fees and make a decision as to whether you would be better off paying them separately if you can.

"What might change the interest rate and what notice will I receive?"

If you opt for a rate that is not fixed, it is useful to know how often your interest rates will be reviewed and whether any relationship to the Bank of England base rate might change your payments.

"What if I repay my mortgage early?"

Early repayment charges may apply if you repay the mortgage in the early years. Make sure you understand how much you would have to pay.

"Would I be charged if I made extra payments?"

Early repayment charges can be charged if you pay off any monies over and above your regular monthly mortgage payments (see page 47). Alternatively, you may be able to pay off a certain amount extra each month or year.

"What if my circumstances change?"

Your adviser will have full knowledge of how any changes in your circumstances may affect your ability to pay your mortgage or associated protection policies, and should indicate how flexible the lender can be.

"Can I take the mortgage with me if I move?"

You should be able to do so but there may be conditions attached. Your mortgage lender or financial adviser should tell you of any restrictions.

"What if I miss or am late with a payment?"

Lenders must have a written policy on this issue and make clear any charges for falling into arrears. Check what these are before you agree to the mortgage.

"How long will it take to process my application?"

This could be really important if you've already had an offer accepted on a property. Most lenders will give you a Mortgage Agreement in Principle (MAP) within minutes (see page 40) but it can then take from a few weeks to six weeks for a mortgage lender to confirm their offer.

WHAT YOU NEED WHEN ARRANGING A MORTGAGE

A mortgage is a loan of a massive amount of money (not that you ever see it) so obviously the lender will need to check who you are and your financial details. When you go to a mortgage interview you will need:

- **Proof of identity,** such as a driving licence, utility bill or passport.
- **Proof of income** – three recent payslips or your latest P60. Bringing a letter from your employer confirming your earnings will save time as the lender will ask for this.
- **Your bank account** details.
- **Your current mortgage** account number and amount outstanding.
- **Any other addresses** you have lived at, if you haven't lived in your own property for three years or more.

❝A mortgage is a loan of a large amount of money so the lender must check your financial details. ❞

It would also be useful if you have:

- **Evidence** of your expenditure (such as the table on page 27). This will show you are serious about buying and have thought about what you can realistically afford.
- **Proof** of where you live (such as two recent utility bills).

- **Information** about the property you are selling.
- **Details of the property** you would like to buy, assuming you actually know this.

KEY FACTS ILLUSTRATIONS (KFI)

Once you have decided on which mortgage you want or your adviser has recommended one to you, your adviser will then provide a summary of the mortgage. The key facts illustration provides details of the features, terms and conditions of the mortgage in a standardised format, so it should enable you to compare different lenders' products on the same basis. It is personalised to you and the amount you want to borrow.

Among other things, the key facts illustration will tell you:

- The overall cost of the mortgage
- How much your regular payments will be
- The initial interest rate and what it will rise to after any special deal ends
- Whether there are any penalties for overpaying
- What happens if you repay the mortgage early or move house
- Whether there are any conditional products that you must buy, such as insurance
- If it's a variable rate mortgage, it will also include an illustration of the amount by which your regular payments would increase if the base rate were to rise by 1 per cent.

HOW TO AVOID GETTING BAD ADVICE

Following the regulation of advice and sale of products by the FSA, getting the right information about mortgages and related financial products should be easier and more professional. Here are some hints and tips to make sure that you steer clear of all bad advice that may still be out there!

- **Work out your monthly budget** so that you know how much you can afford to pay, allowing for changes in interest rates (see page 36).
- **Be clear about your attitude to risk:** do you mind the prospect of costs going up as well as down, or prefer the reassurance of knowing exactly what you'll be paying each month?
- **Go to an independent mortgage adviser** unless you are very confident that you know exactly what you want. They can recommend any mortgage or service on the market, rather than tied advisers, who only sell their own company's loans, or advisers who only offer a selection of lenders and their products. To find an independent mortgage adviser, see the box at the foot of page 51.
- **If you get advice from a mortgage lender,** you will have to compare the cost of rival mortgages yourself, which can be time-consuming and confusing as you will not always be comparing like with like.

Independent financial advisers and brokers should do this for you.

- **Choose the 'advised' level of service,** rather than the 'information only' level (see page 50), which puts all the responsibility for the final choice onto you. Check this on the initial disclosure document (IDD) (see page 51), which should be produced right at the start of the meeting.
- **Ask questions** about anything you do not understand (it is the adviser's job to make it clear) and compare costs by monthly payment and total cost over the time you expect to keep the mortgage loan for.
- **Get costings** on different mortgage terms such as 15, 25 and 30 years. Longer loans mean lower monthly payments but a higher repayment to the lender over the term of the mortgage.
- **Tell your adviser** if you think you'll by able to make overpayments or pay the loan off early: it will affect the choice of mortgage deal.
- **Be clear** about what is being recommended, its cost implications, the fees and charges involved. Study the KFI and check you understand it or ask your adviser if you have any more questions.

 If you think you were advised badly, you may have grounds for a mis-selling complaint - see overleaf.

Surf and save

It is well worth checking out mortgage deals on the internet, even if it is only to be reassured that you have got a reasonable deal. The best thing to do is to go to a mortgage calculator (such as www.switchwithwhich.co.uk or www.moneysupermarket.co.uk), and fill out the relevant forms online.

- **Ask your adviser** why he or she is recommending this deal and make sure that you are given a satisfactory rationale that is appropriate for your circumstances.
- **Think about your finances** and decide how important it would be to have a flexible mortgage where you can overpay or take a holiday (see pages 45–6), or whether you don't mind payments varying, or if your priority is to keep costs down in the short-term when you may be more strapped for cash.

Badly advised?

If you think you were badly advised, go to the firm who advised you (they will be named in the initial disclosure document) and ask for a copy of their complaints procedure. Follow the procedure, but if the issue is not resolved to your satisfaction, go to the Financial Ombudsman Service (FOS). They will investigate your complaint and make a binding adjudication, which is only binding on the lender, not on you. If you don't accept this adjudication, your only recourse is going to court. Contact the FOS via www.financial ombudsman.org.uk or on 0845 080 1800.

❝Choose the 'advised' level of service rather than the 'information only' level, which puts all the responsibility for the final choice onto you. Check this on the IDD. **❞**

Mortgage problems

It is possible that something happens when you are buying or have bought your home that means you realise you may be in a position where you either can't get a mortgage, or once you have one, you can't afford to pay it. This section helps to explain why you might be rejected for a mortgage, what you can do about it and what to do if you get into trouble.

GETTING A MORTGAGE

There are a number of reasons why it can be difficult to get a mortgage. These are the main ones.

No deposit

Most lenders prefer not to lend 100 per cent of the property value because of the risk of not getting their money back if you default on the payments and they have to repossess the property. However, some lenders are prepared to loan the full amount (see page 29).

Self-employed

The self-employed or those with irregular incomes cannot always provide the financial information to reassure a lender that they are safe to lend to. Again, some lenders are happy to lend under these circumstances (see page 32).

Retiring soon

Many people opt to downsize their home when they no longer need lots of space and spare rooms. If you still need a mortgage when downsizing and nearing retirement, you may be restricted on the loan period or the amount they will lend you.

❝If you have a poor credit record but you maintain regular payments on your chosen mortgage, you may be able to re-negotiate more favourable terms after three years. ❞

Poor credit record

When you apply for a mortgage, the lender is likely to run checks with credit reference agencies. They are basically looking to find out what your credit history is like, in other words, if you have a history of bad debts or property repossessions. You can check the information held on you with the main agencies via www.experian.co.uk, www.equifax.co.uk and www.callcredit.co.uk. This is well worth doing as the information they hold can be inaccurate or out of date (see page 32). A specialist broker or lender may still be able to help to get you a mortgage, although you are likely to be charged higher interest rates. If you maintain regular payments, you may be able to re-negotiate more favourable terms after three years.

 If a lender rejects your application, find out why and then talk to an experienced independent mortgage adviser, if you haven't already. However, remember you will have to inform them that a previous application has been refused. Double-check that you haven't been turned down due to credit reference issues or other information on your paperwork that may not be accurate (see page 32).

Low income

You may be able to join a home ownership scheme run by a local council or housing association. Examples include:

- **The Right to Buy** scheme in which occupiers can purchase the property they are renting from the council.
- **The Right to Acquire** scheme for housing association tenants.
- **Shared ownership,** in which you pay a mortgage and rent and share the ownership of the property with your local housing association.
- **The starter homes initiative** for key workers, such as teachers, health workers and police officers, which offers interest-free loans and shared ownership deals. Schemes are mostly run by a housing association, council or NHS trust.
- **The Homebuy** scheme, which aims to help council and housing association tenants buy property on the open market.

❝ If you are on a low income there are several schemes that may be able to help you. ❞

 For more information on how to afford a property while on a low income, go to these websites: www.shelter.org.uk and www.housingcorp.co.uk. See also pages 139–41, which explain what options are available to you.

Problems with the property

The lender may be reluctant to loan on properties in a poor state of repair, short leases, unusual houses or flats (such as being located over a shop), or houses made of unusual materials, even thatched properties. There are, however, lenders who are willing to lend on 'non-standard' properties. For properties in a poor state of repair, try www.buildstore.co.uk. For other, non-standard properties, also look at the buildstore website or www.ecology.co.uk.

❝ There are specialist lenders who are willing to lend on 'non-standard' properties. ❞

Fair enough?

All lenders are now regulated by the FSA, whose rules state they must 'deal fairly with any customer who is in arrears'. They must have a written policy on arrears, set up a feasible payment plan for you, and update you regularly on your arrears without applying pressure with excessive telephone calls or letters. However, you must make every effort to keep up with the new payment plan.

WHAT TO DO IF YOU CAN'T AFFORD TO PAY YOUR MORTGAGE

There are many reasons why people can hit difficulties in meeting their monthly mortgage payment, such as long-term illness, birth of a child, relationship breakdown or unemployment.

If you are having trouble meeting mortgage payments, the first course of action should be to tell your lender. It is in their interest to help you out rather than instigate an expensive and time-consuming repossession on your property.

Don't forget that if you don't sort out the issues and payments with your lender, you wouldn't just lose your home, but it would also be very difficult for you to get any more loans or a mortgage again.

It may be that you can get help with your mortgage payments. Remember that your lender will want to help you solve the problem now, rather than allow things to get worse. If you aren't getting much help from a local office, then contact their head office. Check, too, to see if you have got any cover, such as accident, sickness and unemployment or critical illness cover (see page 49) that may pay out for you.

Arrangements that a mortgage lender may offer you in order to help you during difficulties making mortgage payments include the various possibilities that are outlined in full overleaf.

Mortgage rescue schemes

This will depend on your lender, but some run this type of scheme. The way in which it works is that your lender could either buy back your home and you become a tenant, or set up a part rent/part buy scheme, known as 'shared ownership'. If your lender doesn't offer this, it may be worth contacting your local housing association as they may be able to help. You can find your local association via the Housing Corporation (www.housingcorp.gov.uk), a government-run body that manages and regulates all the housing associations.

Finally, if you claim benefits, such as income support, pension credit or income-based job seeker's allowance, the Department for Work and Pensions may pay some of the interest on your mortgage to help.

Payment agreement

If you can, offer an extra monthly payment to clear the arrears, probably over 12–24 months, or longer if you do not think this term is feasible. Even if you can't agree an amount with your lender, pay what you can, explaining what you are doing and why. If the value of your home is greater than the outstanding loan on your mortgage, let the lender know as you may be able to re-mortgage and pay back the arrears over the lifetime of the mortgage.

Adding the arrears to your mortgage

The mortgage is re-negotiated with the arrears added to the total loan, spreading the cost over the remaining years of the mortgage term. This would increase your monthly mortgage payments, but help spread the cost of the arrears over a longer period of time so you don't have to find a large lump sum to pay.

Extend the mortgage term

The standard term for a mortgage is 25 years but lenders may consider increasing this by five or ten years. It may also be that you only have 15 or 20 years left on your current

❝ If you do sell your property and still owe money to the lender, make sure you come to an arrangement where you can continue to afford to pay off the monies. ❞

 If you have payment problems, contact National Debtline (www.nationaldebtline.co.uk); http://england.shelter.org.uk, website of the charity Shelter; www.clsdirect.org.uk, website of the Community Legal Service; www.cccs.co.uk, website for the Consumer Credit Counselling Service and/or www.citizensadvice.org.uk.

mortgage, so it would be easier to extend the payment to 25 years. This would bring down the cost of your monthly payments, but don't forget that in the long-term you would be paying more back because of the additional interest charges over the extra term.

Paying interest only

Your lender may accept a monthly payment covering only the interest on your mortgage for a short period of time, which may help you sort out your finances and return to paying a repayment mortgage or continuing to pay your savings plan if you have an interest-only mortgage.

If you can't cover the mortgage in any way

You may decide or be advised that you can't cover the mortgage on any terms. Some people just hand in the keys, but this doesn't mean you don't owe the lender money any more. In fact, you will still be charged the monthly instalments on the mortgage. Any debts you accrue from this will be added with interest to what you owe. Then, when the house is sold, the lenders' legal fees, the estate agent's fees and any court costs that are incurred when trying to recover monies from you will be added to the monies owed.

Another alternative is to sell your property to cover your debts, repay the mortgage lender and move to a cheaper, smaller home, or look at

renting from a housing association if you are eligible. It may also be possible to rent out the home for a while – if this means you can pay the bills. You may even be able to move in with friends or relatives for a short time to help you get over a short-term financial problem.

If you do sell your property and still owe money to the lender, make sure you come to an arrangement where you can continue to afford to pay off the monies.

Can't pay? Do say!

The four steps to deal with this problem are:

1 Explain the difficulty to your lender.
2 Pay what you can.
3 Look for ways to increase your income.
4 Sell the property and pay off your debts.

Insuring your home

Insurance is a vital part of protecting your home and belongings. There are two kinds of insurance that you will need to look into.

- Buildings insurance covers the cost of rebuilding your home if it is damaged. You won't be able to exchange on a property until this is organised.
- Contents insurance covers your possessions. It is not compulsory and about a quarter of UK households don't have it. They are taking a big risk.

Many mortgage lenders also sell contents and buildings insurance, but it is always worth shopping around to get the best deal and some companies can offer much better rates than your incumbent lender. There are also some circumstances that may require specialist insurance – for example, if you work from home and need to cover all of your business equipment, or if you have a thatched cottage.

❝ As a rough guide, the cost of rebuilding a home is approximately 75 per cent of its value, but the insurance company will verify this for you. ❞

BUILDINGS INSURANCE

The sum insured must be enough to pay for the cost of rebuilding your home if it is severely damaged by fire, storms, flooding or other catastrophes. This is usually lower than the value of your property because it only covers the bricks and mortar and labour to rebuild your property, not the cost of the land. As a rough guide, the cost of rebuilding a home is approximately 75 per cent of its value, but the insurance company will verify this for you. If you want guidance on the figure, a surveyor should be able to help and you can use online calculators too (see www.abi.org.uk). Insurers will need to know various details about the property including:

- What year it was built.
- Type of construction, such as brick and tile construction, or 19th-century stone, or timber framed houses.
- Postcode of the property to check for flooding or other environmental risks (see page 147).
- How many bedrooms/rooms the property has.

At risk of flood?

Two million homes in England and Wales are at risk of flooding, 40 per cent of these are classified as a high risk at a time when our climate is changing. Insurers will assess your risk of flooding from your postcode and other information they have. However, different insurers can consider different postcodes as high or low risk, depending on the information they have. For example, if you live near a river but are on a hill, your risk of flooding is a lot less than someone in the same postcode at the bottom of the hill. Your insurer may not take this into account though as some insurers use full postcodes, some don't. Depending on the insurer, you may get a cheaper or more expensive quote. Many companies are refusing to insure new customers who have made a flooding claim in the past. However, all insurance companies who are members of the Association of British Insurers have signed up to a statement of principles, which lays out how the insurance companies could possibly help residential properties that are on a floodplain.

What the insurance covers

Buildings insurance covers the reconstruction of your home, including fixtures and fittings, if it is destroyed or damaged by anything out of your control such as:

- Subsidence.
- Storm and flood damage.
- Burst pipes and other water leaks.
- Fire, smoke and explosions (excluding acts of war or terrorism).
- Vandalism or third-party damage.

❝ Do not assume every policy covers every possibility. Read the small print and if you are not clear on anything, ask the insurer. ❞

Cover usually includes the basic structure plus all windows, the roof, kitchen and bathroom floors, electrical wiring and plumbing. External constructions, such as a conservatory, shed, garage or greenhouse, are also generally covered. Do not assume every policy covers every possibility. As always, read the small print and if you are not clear on a point, ask the insurer or your broker.

Consider the level of cover you need. Never under insure your possessions, but also don't pay more than you have to by over insuring. An

Any flood defence measures in your area may help you get a better deal with an insurance company. The following sites will help identify if the property is at risk from flooding: www.environment-agency.gov.uk and www.homecheck.co.uk.

unlimited policy may be worth looking at if you have a lot of things that have a high value, which may nevertheless need to be insured separately.

In your research it is worth checking these points:

- **Do you have the right level** of cover? Make sure everything is taken into account, such as any previous claims or subsidence problems.
- **Do they have a 24-hour** helpline for claims?
- **What would the excess be** and how much less would your insurance cost if you paid a higher excess? (Don't pay monthly as you will pay more – as much as 10–30 per cent.)
- **Would the insurer pay** to house you while your property is being rebuilt or repaired, and what kind of accommodation would it fund and how long for?
- **Would you receive** any interim payments during this period or would they pay costs direct to the supplier?
- **Would you have some input** in the way the house is rebuilt?
- **Would the policy cover** the cost of clearing away any debris and rubble?

If the property you are buying is leasehold, as is the case with most flats, check that the freeholder or managing agent has taken out a buildings insurance policy and if you are liable for part of the cost of this policy. You should ask for a copy of the policy so you can check if you need to take out further insurance, and so that you can supply its detail to your conveyancer and lender before exchanging contracts.

&& Buildings insurance allows for reconstruction of your home, including fixtures and fittings, if it is destroyed or damaged by anything out of your control. ,,

Further information on buildings insurance, including guidance on rebuilding costs, is available from the Association of British Insurers (www.abi.org.uk) and from the Building Cost Information Service (BCIS), part of the Royal Institution of Chartered Surveyors (RICS) – www.bcis.co.uk – and www.which.co.uk.

- **Are architects** and surveyors or other fees included?
- **How long** does it usually take to assess and settle a claim? The company should be able to give you a guideline.

CONTENTS INSURANCE

This provides protection for your possessions inside the home if they are damaged, destroyed or stolen. It can also cover things outside the house, if you pay extra and as long as they aren't taken off the property altogether. It should include just about everything you would take with you if you moved home – furniture and furnishings, household goods, kitchen equipment, televisions, DVD and video players, computer and audio equipment, clothing, personal effects, and valuables up to stated limits.

When taking out a policy you will be asked about:

- **Whether you are leaving** the property unoccupied during the day.

- **If you are out of the country** for long periods (more than a month or two).
- **What security devices** are fitted, e.g. an alarm.
- **Your employment.**
- **Past house insurance** claims.
- **If you have a criminal** record.
- **Your postcode,** which insurers use to calculate the level of risk and which can significantly influence the premium.
- **Any other factor** that influences the security or risk of damage to your items, such as if you are self-employed and regularly take a laptop or other expensive equipment away with you.

Level of cover

Most policies set a limit on the overall amount you can claim, known as the **'sum insured'.** Some insurers stick to a set sum assured (usually about £30,000), others are happy to customise the policy to your needs, while some give **unlimited cover.**

Working out the value of your possessions is a time-consuming but essential process, although you don't have to go into so much detail if your policy is **bedroom rated** (see jargon buster box, overleaf). You need to tour every room noting down everything in it and estimating what its cost is worth. Keep receipts for valuable items as a record and even take photographs. It is advisable to get an expert valuation on any unusual valuables, art or antiques, so that you

Moving?

If you are selling your house, keep the insurance cover in place until you have completed. Then you can cancel it and may be able to claim a refund on any monies outstanding if you have not made a claim that year. Alternatively, you could, of course, transfer the policy to your new home.

know you have it insured for the right amount. It is important to review your sum insured regularly, at least once a year, to allow for the cost of any items you purchase.

> **❝ It is a wise precaution to get an expert valuation on any unusual valuables. ❞**

It is generally agreed in the insurance industry that most people under value their possessions. If this is proved to be the case, your insurer will only pay out the amount or less you insured with them, rather than the true item value. So if you insure for £50K and the property is worth £100K and you claim for £50K, you will only get 50 per cent of this, which equals £25K. Make sure your policy is updated on an annual basis.

The website of the Association of British Insurers (www.abi.org.uk) has a free spreadsheet you can download to help you calculate how much your contents are worth. Go to the consumer section within the 'information zone' on their website.

Replacement as new versus indemnity cover

Most companies only insure new for old, although some offer indemnity cover as well.

Replacement as new (also known as new for old)

This pays the full cost of repairing or replacing damaged or lost articles with brand new ones. Most policies exclude clothing and household linen. Sometimes age limits also apply.

❝Ensure high value items are specifically listed and take a photo of them.❞

High-value items

If you have some high-value items you have several options:

- Ensure they are specifically listed in the policy with their value, and photograph them.
- Insure them separately (for example, some insurers specialise in musical instrument or cycle cover) or add them to your policy for a charge.
- Break down the item into component parts of lower value (such as the separate parts of a hi-fi system, or the lenses, main body and peripherals of a camera).

Indemnity cover

This makes a deduction in the value to allow for wear and tear and depreciation, so premiums will be cheaper – but you'll only get the second-hand value of your possessions. Because of this you may be asked, and need to prove the year, in which certain items were acquired.

Your responsibilities

You are expected to keep the insured possessions in a good state of repair and take all reasonable steps to prevent loss or damage occurring to them. Most policies will cover loss or damage to your possessions while in your home by:

- Fire, explosion, lightning or earthquake
- Subsidence, heave or landslip
- Storm and flood
- Theft or attempted theft
- Escape of water from tanks or pipes
- Falling trees or branches
- Breakage or collapse of television, radio signal or satellite apparatus
- Riot, civil commotion, strikes, labour or political disturbances
- Impact by aircraft, other aerial devices, any vehicle or animal
- Escape of oil from heating systems.

Policies can be extended to cover **accidental damage** to or loss of items that you may take out of your home. This can cover such items as clothing, jewellery, cameras and sports equipment (which you might also decide to insure on an **all-risk basis**, so they are covered away from your home). Further cover can be arranged to insure personal money and credit cards, cycles and legal expenses. If you extend a policy, your premium may go up, so it is worth shopping around to see if you can get a better deal. You will also pay a higher premium if you opt for cover for possessions outside of the home.

You may be required to pay the first part of a claim yourself (from £50 to £500 or so) – this is called the 'excess'. Excesses are applied to a range of claims and you can set the excess to be higher or lower, which may decrease or increase the monthly or annual premium. The level of discount will increase with the size of excess you choose: the higher the excess, the lower your premium. Also note that subsidence excess can be much higher – ranging from £1,000 to £2,000.

> ** The level of discount will increase with the size of excess you choose: the higher the excess, the lower the premium. Subsidence excess can be much higher. **

Moving house?

Remember to notify your current contents insurers of the date of your move. However, if the move is going to take more than a day to be completed, get them to hold the cover on both addresses.

Check also if the policy covers your possessions during the move, as this is a time when things can be easily damaged. If it doesn't cover them, ask your removal company if they have insurance that will cover your possessions during the move (see page 167).

Your policy will exclude certain risks or possessions. Common exclusions are theft if you have let or sub-let your house (or part of it), unless there is forced entry, or loss or damage arising if you leave your house unoccupied for long periods (typically, more than 30 days).

Other things that you need to consider are:

- **Whether the policy covers** accidental damage (there is usually an extra charge for this).
- **Are valuables** insured in transit and while you are on holiday?
- **If the policy covers** any lost or stolen cash and if there is a limit on the amount.
- **See also the checklist** on buildings insurance (page 66).

HOW MUCH YOU'LL PAY

Premiums on buildings and contents policies change every year, so you can save money by shopping around annually. The buildings element is usually index-linked to the retail price index so a series of natural disasters can increase the price of your policy, as can several years of high claim levels. The number of years that you have not made a claim for also makes a difference to your premium. The more years you haven't claimed for the better, as you can get a no claims discount up to a maximum percentage. You can also keep your costs as low as possible by:

- **Shopping around** for the best deal and insurance package to suit your specific needs.
- **Buying buildings and contents insurance** as a package, which reduces administration overheads and prevents a dispute between two insurers about who should pay a claim.
- **Being careful** not to over or under insure the building or contents.
- **Avoiding paying** for cover you don't need. For example, if you haven't got a garage, ensure you aren't paying for one.
- **Agree to pay an excess**, such as the first £200 of any claim (the standard excess is £50). Paying a larger excess can reduce premiums.
- **Fit good locks** to doors and especially windows and other entry points to a property. Ask if your insurer stipulates certain kinds or standard of locks, or gives a discount if they are in place. The Association of British Insurers (www.abi.org.uk) recommends that outside doors have a five-lever mortice deadlock with a steel striking plate, which conforms to BS3621.
- **Join a neighbourhood watch** scheme. This can earn a discount of up to 15 per cent.
- **If at all possible**, pay the premium straightaway. Opting for monthly payments can incur higher charges over the year – sometimes adding up to 30 per cent on to the premium.

> **❝Shop around annually for buildings and contents policies as premiums change. Consider buying them as a package as this reduces administration overheads. ❞**

 For websites that offer you insurance comparisons, check out the following website addresses: www.insuresupermarket.com, www.confused.com and www.1stquote.co.uk.

WHERE TO GO

Many companies in this field exploit the easy-going consumer who does not research the market. Insurance is often an add-on to other discussions about, say, mortgages, and you may be reluctant to hold up proceedings by shopping around at this stage. This is a mistake. Bank or lender insurance premiums can be significantly higher than those of the other 9,000 brokers operating in a highly competitive market. Do not rely on your mortgage provider to give you the best deal. So make sure you shop around!

HOW TO COMPARE INSURANCE QUOTES

In your research for insurance it is important that you try to compare quotes that are like with like so that you are looking at the whole deal and not just the price. If you have the time, consider doing all the research online, although you should remember that the internet is not comprehensive. Most insurers have their own websites, but, of course, these only cover their own policies. A broker will be able to choose from a wider selection, or there are many insurance comparison sites that search more widely than anyone else (for some examples, see box, below).

 Once you have purchased your insurance, you will be sent a copy of the policy. While it is tempting to file it away, read it first to check the accuracy of the details and ensure it covers everything agreed. Keep the policy where you can retrieve it easily in case of an urgent claim.

❝In your research for insurance it is important to compare quotes that are like with like so that you are looking at the whole deal and not just the price.❞

Bear in mind that no one site is comprehensive and it can be difficult to know if you are comparing like with like: you'll need to check policy details with the provider when you are close to making your choice.

 Websites that can provide you with detailed information for all the subjects covered in this section are the Financial Services Authority (www.fsa.gov.uk), the Financial Ombudsman Service (www.financial-ombudsman.org.uk) and www.which.co.uk.

Valuing a property

A common mistake is to try to buy or sell property without understanding the market. In this crucial, life-changing process, it is vital that you have some understanding of the national conditions, and the vagaries of your local market. Only then can you compare like with like and make informed decisions about what a home is worth.

Understanding the market

If we were to believe all the press reports and media spin about property prices, we would think there is only one property market. If the press says property prices have risen by 10 per cent, then all property prices have risen by 10 per cent.

The problem with this is that the next week another report might say that property prices have stayed the same, or even fallen. As a result, it is difficult to understand what is happening to property prices in the 'market' - this is because there isn't just 'one' property market. Property prices are dependent on many factors. Prices across the country tend to vary according to the general state of the economy and how confident people are about their job prospects, and therefore their attitude to buying and selling a home. They also depend on how many properties are on the market and how many people want to buy. However, the key point in understanding property prices is that they are mostly influenced by local factors, not national ones.

Although property prices to go up or down across the country as a whole, the 'property market' covers between 1.2 and 1.5 million homes.

❝ The same property can vary in price from one month to the next, depending on how many buyers there are and how many other similar properties there are for sale in the area. ❞

Some of these properties might be brand new flats in one area, others might be old character properties. Some local economies might be expanding, others might be suffering from loss of a major employer. Depending on the number of buyers and sellers of flats or old properties, then prices in each of these areas could be going up or down – and at the same time.

 To understand the market even more, it is important to compare property prices - see pages 83-8. If you are buying a property, see also pages 124-32 for information on the different types.

The other important factor to understand about property prices is that the same property can vary in price from one month to the next. This all depends on how many buyers there are and how many other similar properties there are for sale in the area.

WHY PRICES CAN VARY

Imagine the scenario that you put your three-bedroomed house with a garage and garden up for sale. At the time you put your property on the market, there are few other similar properties available and lots of people are looking to buy one like yours. As a result, your estate agent puts it on the market at what they believe is a maximum price of £185,000. You get two or three offers and maybe there is even a **bidding war** and you end up getting £187,000 for your property.

Two months later your neighbour – whose property is the same as yours and decorated to the same standard – puts their property on the market and, seeing your price, the estate agent suggests a price of £190,000, hoping to get £187,000. However, by now, others in your locality have put their properties up for sale and there is some competition. One of the sellers needs to move urgently so their home is priced at £180,000 for a 'quick sale'. Suddenly the price for the neighbour's property looks high, and there is more choice, so to sell the property even a few months after you have, they may have to accept several thousand pounds less than you did.

&& Be careful not to use property price surveys as a guide to an 'average house price'. There is actually no such thing when it comes to property surveys. 99

Valuing a property

Jargon buster

Asking price Price a seller hopes to achieve

Bidding war When more than one party is interested in buying a property and so they bid up the price

Property price survey Research that shows the prices of properties across the country

Selling price Price actually achieved, can be lower or higher than the asking price

USING PROPERTY PRICE SURVEYS

One useful tool for assessing the overall upward or downward trend in property prices is the **property price surveys**, which are compiled by various companies. However, you must be careful not to use them as a guide to an 'average house price'. We often witness the media quoting property price surveys, which talk about an 'average house price'. You may think this refers to a three-bedroomed semi and that the surveys compare the cost of this type of property across the country, but this is not the case. There is actually no such thing as an 'average' property when it comes to property price surveys.

What the property price surveys typically quote as an 'average property price' is a sum of all the properties they have in their database from which they obtain their 'average' price. However, some surveys include property that is sold for over £1 million while others don't. Some only cover mortgaged properties and omit those that might be sold and are owned outright, lowering the average property price that they quote versus other surveys.

They also vary so widely because they measure the market at different times of the property sale. For example, Rightmove measures the asking prices, whereas the Land Registry measures prices at the end of the transaction after any

negotiations have taken place at survey or mortgage offer stage, which means they can be significantly lower. In addition, some surveys only cover England and Wales while others cover the whole of the UK, including Scotland and Northern Ireland.

The real value of property price surveys is to banks and other financial analysts who use them to assess consumer spending trends and the state of the economy. They also help the property services, such as estate agents and surveyors, to understand the impact on their business at a national level and to plan their staffing, sales and marketing initiatives.

To the general public, property price surveys can be helpful in providing information on how long it might take to buy or sell a property, whether the market is active and therefore you will have to make decisions more quickly,

> **❝ Property price surveys can be helpful in providing information on how long it might take to buy or sell a property. They tell you whether the market is active or slow at that time. ❞**

Other sources for getting hold of local property market information are local newspapers, local estate agents and the internet. Each of these areas are explored on pages 84-6.

or if it is slow and you can therefore take your time. So effectively it gives a feel for how buyers are likely to react when you put your property up for sale. However, what surveys don't do is let you know what price you should market your property for, how much it has gone up (or down) in value since you last bought it, or how much you should offer. This depends on what is happening in the local market and the demand and supply for the property you are buying or selling. Property price survey information is available from:

Rightmove

This company has the widest range of all these surveys, collating information from more than 500,000 property sale details at any one time. The figures that they use only quote the 'asking price' or 'advertised price' for a property and so they can overestimate the real prices achieved. For example, if a property is advertised at £300,000 but sells for £285,000, Rightmove will quote the higher figure. They release their data on a monthly basis and you can access the information at www.rightmove.co.uk.

Hometrack

Hometrack analyses data from over 3,000 estate agents in England and Wales. It is widely regarded as the most useful survey because it compares **asking prices** with actual **selling prices** as well as assessing the demand and supply of properties in the area.

❝ The main property price surveys are Rightmove, Hometrack, the Halifax, Nationwide, the Royal Institute of Chartered Surveyors, the National Association of Estate Agents and the Land Registry. ❞

It also gives the average number of viewings for each sale and the average time a property is on the market. This helps you to understand whether you are getting enough viewings to sell your home and whether you are behind your local market when it comes to selling. If you are buying, it also helps you to see how fast or slowly the market is moving. Hometrack sorts data by postcode. The downside is that you need to pay for this service to assess the local market and the value of your own property. It costs from £5 to £20. Hometrack does, however, release its general information on a monthly

 While property price surveys are helpful for assessing the market, you need the assistance of an estate agent when it comes to actually valuing your own property. For more information, see pages 93-7.

they are still valuable for showing national and regional price movements, and both allow you to put a price on your own property using their 'trend' data to estimate how much it is worth now versus when you bought it. However, it is only a guide, so don't rely on it.

Their information is released on a monthly basis for national information and a quarterly basis for regional information and can be accessed by visiting their websites: www.nationwide.co.uk/hpi and www.hbosplc.com/economy/housingresearch.asp.

RICS and the NAEA

The Royal Institution of Chartered Surveyors (RICS) measures data supplied by its 350+ surveyors and its prices take into account the condition of the property. The National Association of Estate Agents (NAEA) gives a good idea of the current supply and demand by showing how many properties agents have on their books. The higher this number, the harder properties will be to sell unless they really stand out.

Both organisations release information each month and you can access this by visiting their websites: www.naea.co.uk and www.rics.org.

basis and you can access this and press release data via their website at www.hometrack.co.uk.

Halifax and Nationwide

Both of these companies take data from their mortgage lending businesses and so do not include the 25 per cent of property sales achieved without mortgages. Nevertheless,

The Land Registry

This survey covers actual transactions and the final price that someone pays for a property. Although this information is the most accurate of all the data and surveys, the problem for buyers and sellers is that it is only released on a quarterly basis. So, as house prices can go up and down over a month, let alone three months, the Land Registry data is not especially helpful when you are buying and selling as it quickly becomes too historic and out of date.

UNDERSTANDING YOUR LOCAL PROPERTY MARKET

Understanding the local market for a property you want to buy or sell is far more important than any media reports on property price movements. There are many factors that can influence what is happening to property prices and how much you should offer or sell a property for.

❝ Understanding the local market for a property that you want to buy or sell is far more important than any media reports you might read on property price movements. **❞**

Location

Local property markets are sub-divided into many sectors. For example, some streets are valued highly because they are adjacent to a park and so appeal to families with young children, or have plenty of parking, or are lined with beautiful trees. Others are worth less to some people because they have a pub that is notoriously noisy or the street is often strewn with litter from fast food outlets. As a result, it is important to understand the market and property type that you wish to buy or sell in your local area. For example, is there an over- or under-supply of old or new properties? What about easy access to shops? If there are only a few shops, then it is likely that properties within walking distance will be more expensive than those you have to drive from. Any properties on main or busy/noisy roads, for example, are likely to be cheaper than those set away from a road or in a quiet, idyllic location.

One of the biggest reasons for property price differences at a local level is the performance of schools. In some cases, property prices can be between 19 and 34 per cent higher than other areas due to a good school catchment area. However, be aware

❝One of the biggest reasons for property price differences at a local level is the performance of schools. In some cases, property prices can be between 19 and 34 per cent higher than other areas due to a good school catchment area. ❞

that not all local authorities and their schools have the same catchment area each year. Some vary the area according to local demand. The school may also be full and not accepting any new pupils, so if you are hoping to buy a property in a postcode to 'guarantee' a place for your children at a school, check with the school directly.

Economic

Is the area that you are buying or selling in expanding or contracting? For example, are companies moving into or out of the area? Are shops closing down due to lack of business or are they being turned into trendy

outdoor cafés suggesting a new breed of professionals moving into the area?

Another good sign of economic development is if new properties are being built locally. Are the major house builders moving in? Are new estate agents opening up in the area? Perhaps there are run-down parts that are now being bought up and turned into hotels, entertainment centres or executive flats.

These elements are not guaranteed to turn an area around or boost the property market in the long run, but they are definitely signs that things are on the up or down and therefore help you to understand whether prices are likely to rise or fall.

Transport links

Investment in local transport movements can impact dramatically on an area's fortune. For example, a new road or rail or tram link that means access to a major city or area of work may cut down travel from an hour to half an hour. Alternatively, lack of investment in transport and increased congestion can reduce prices as people try to move nearer to other modes of transport, or indeed decide to leave the area and live and work somewhere else.

Types of property and local demand

Each area will have new properties, flats, detached, semi-detached and terraced homes. Unfortunately, there is likely to be a glut of some properties and an under-supply of others. For example, over the last few years, developers have been building many flats and apartments for city centres. These have been snapped up by some first-time or second-time buyers, and many by investors. Now that these investors have turned their sights abroad to gain the returns they want, in some areas, the demand for these properties isn't as high as it was.

Character and old properties, particularly in idyllic country village locations that are still near to major towns or cities with good jobs, are always likely to be in short supply as many people want to live in them, but, unfortunately, supply cannot be increased. Hence some developers are trying to build properties with the 'character' of old ones, but the benefits of new builds.

Whenever you are looking to buy or sell a particular property in an area, make sure you talk to the local estate agents and surveyors and ask them what is the demand and supply for the type of property you are looking for or selling. In this way, you know that if demand is high, you will have to be prepared to offer more, or make a quick decision for a property you want to buy. Conversely, if demand is low and slow, you may have to take time and be patient in selling your home.

Local factors

There may be other factors locally that affect property prices, such as an area becoming well known for drug dealing, or indeed drug dealers being chased out of the area. We have already discussed the major impact that a good school can have on the price of property. However, it may be that a 'badly scored' school takes on a new head who over a few years turns the school around, which is likely to impact positively on the price of property in the area.

Some areas are well known, too, for problems with flooding, subsidence or radon. If you are not local, then always read the local newspapers as they will typically mention this over the time you are looking to purchase a property. If you are local, then you are likely to know which areas are affected and can make your own decision on how big an issue you feel it might be. Always check what effect this will have on your ability to get, or the cost of, insurance as an

❝ Make sure you talk to local estate agents and surveyors and ask them what is the demand and supply for the type of property you are looking for or selling. **❞**

For further information on facts that affect the local property market, see these websites: www.environment-agency.gov.uk (environmental); www.homecheck.co.uk and www.upmystreet.com (crime).

insurer won't always cover you (see pages 64–6).

Increasingly, crime has an impact on an area's price, but do check whether this is media hype or a real problem. One serious break-in, or worse, doesn't mean the whole place is awful to live in; it may have been a one-off occurrence. To get a sense of how much of an issue this is, check crime statistics or talk to the local police.

66 The better you understand the local area, the better you will be able to understand what might help you sell your home or if it is worth buying in that area. 99

Insurance companies are worth talking to as well, as they will increase/decrease premiums according to the local crime rate. This can be particularly helpful if you are comparing two different properties in different postcode areas, as you may find the costs of insuring one property versus another are very different.

All of these factors will affect whether the price of property in the area is growing more or less than the average property prices quoted by the media. The better you understand these dynamics, the better you will be able to understand what might help you sell your home or if it is worth buying a property in an area.

Comparing property prices

Even though local factors can affect property prices going up or down, the demand and supply of individual types of properties in that area can also cause the price of one property on one street to go up and the price on another to go down on a street a few metres away.

To explain how these prices can vary dramatically from one road to another, the table below shows how three different three-bedroomed semi-detached properties (new, Victorian and one built in the 1950s) will vary in price according to demand and supply and their appeal to people with contrasting requirements.

The new property could be worth around £180,000, the Victorian property around £220,000 as it is a character property and in short supply, while the 1950s property might fetch around £160,000 as it's ex-local authority and some of the nearby properties are still social housing. All these properties could be within a few hundred metres of each other, yet the price difference for the same 'three-bedroomed property' could vary by over 35 per cent.

Comparison chart for different styles of property

Properties with the same number of bedrooms (in this example, three), in the same area, can appeal to different markets, based on age and facilities.

Age	History/style	Location	Parking	Potential market
New	• Small terraced property	• Suburban estate	• Two spaces allocated	• Working couple, both with company cars, eat out a lot and shop locally
Victorian	• Semi-detached	• Main road	• None	• Non-drivers, possibly a retired couple seeking easy access to public transport, doctors and hospitals
1950s	• Ex-council	• Cul-de-sac	• Garage	• Family with children, keen for them to be able to play safely nearby

In addition, if there are 20 people looking to buy a Victorian semi and there are only three on the market, the prices are likely to rise, while if a new release of 20 three-bed terraced properties are for sale and only five people are looking, the prices are likely to go down.

This example shows how important it is that you assess the property that you want to buy or sell in detail so that you understand why some 'similar' properties sell for more and others for less.

> **"** Even in the age of the internet, local newspapers are by far the easiest way to research the local property market. **"**

SOURCES FOR LOCAL PROPERTY MARKET INFORMATION

To help you find out the demand and supply, and market conditions for a property you are buying or selling, there are many resources that you can now use.

Local newspapers

Even in the age of the internet, local newspapers are by far the easiest way to research the local property market. Some run a weekly report on trends in the area, but just by browsing through the advertisements, watching what sells and what doesn't, you will start to get an idea of what is available and the asking prices.

Look out for properties similar to yours. The asking prices will vary according to the location and condition of each property, but you may be able to make comparisons with your own. Make a note of the maximum and minimum prices properties are selling for and see if they change over a number of weeks (or ideally about three months). Try to work out why some are more expensive than others and how this impacts on the price of your own property. If you have time, have a look at them – you can tell a lot even from

 Increasingly, local newspapers have websites so you can view local news and keep up to date with new properties coming on the market in the area. This is especially valuable if you are moving some distance.

doing a 'drive-by' of the property for sale. Factors affecting the price of individual properties include:

- Quiet location (or not)
- State of repair (paintwork on windows can be a good indicator – old and peeling exterior paintwork suggests lack of maintenance)
- Size of garden
- South-facing gardens are highly prized because they get more sun
- Conservatory
- Parking and/or garage
- What's next door.

Local estate agents

Local estate agents are another useful source of advice, particularly independent agents with a long history in the area. If you are selling, your dealings with them will help you in deciding how best to market your property and which agents offer the most professional service that is right for you (see pages 94–102). They should be able to tell you how long certain properties have been on the market, and how often certain types of property such as yours become available in the area.

If you are buying and show the estate agent that you are not a 'time-waster' (for example, by having a

Mortgage Agreement in Principle ready, or if you are selling a property, already having it on the market), then they will often take time to talk to you about the market and explain the demand and supply for the particular property type that interests you. Try to see them on a day when they aren't too busy, as then they'll spend more time with you.

> **❝ If you are buying and show the estate agent that you are not a 'time-waster', they will often take time to talk to you in detail about the market. ❞**

The internet

A major new resource to research the value of your home – or how much to offer on the property you are looking to buy – is the websites that allow you to find the price that properties have actually sold for in the area you are selling or buying.

This information is only web based, and some charge from £1 per property whereas others allow you to access the information for free, providing you sign up with your email address. See the box below for useful websites.

 The best websites to find figures for what properties have sold at are: www.houseprices.co.uk, www.ourproperty.co.uk and www.rightmove.co.uk. Some websites give access to information for free, others charge you per property.

The advantage such websites have over newspapers is that they will search by postcode and often provide a map showing the location of the property. They also show the price that the property sold for – not what it was advertised at. This is particularly valuable if you have identified certain small areas, even roads, where you would like to buy. It can, however, take up to three months for a particular property's details to appear, but you can look at property sold prices for an individual property up to six months ago to gain an idea of the true value of the type you are selling/looking for.

> **" The advantage of the internet over newspapers is that on appropriate websites you can search by postcode and they often provide a map showing the location of the property. "**

DECIDING WHAT YOUR HOME IS WORTH

The table shown opposite combined with the research already outlined should help you to come up with a reasonable guide as to the value of a property you are going to buy or sell, unless it is a very unusual property with no local 'comparables'. In this case, you will need specialist advice from an estate agent or have to search the 'sold prices' information for a similar property that you know was sold in the last few years. Use the list to itemise the key points about the home you are looking to buy or sell and then compare them with those of similar properties.

Valuations by professionals

As soon as you have a good grasp of what is happening to property prices locally, you can turn to the professionals to help you value your home or sign up with the ones who are likely to sell the type of property you want. Whether or not you are going to use an estate agent (and most people do), it is well worth asking them about the state of the market and how often the property you are selling or buying comes up for sale, and whether it will sell quickly or take some time.

 Further specialist internet property sites are given on page 136. For more information on choosing a suitable agent and getting a valuation, see pages 95–9. These are both important decisions that can't be taken lightly and are the basis of a successful sale.

Property comparison information

Use this list to compare the details of the properties you are most interested in buying or, if you are selling, to make comparisons with your home.

Property price

Total square foot

Property age

e.g. Brand new, post-war, pre-war, pre-1920

Type

e.g. Detached, semi, terraced, flat

Area

e.g. City centre, surburban, rural

Property specification

Number of bedrooms   Extension
Number of reception rooms   Loft conversion
Number of bathrooms   Double-glazing
Conservatory   Central heating

Condition

e.g. Well maintained, some minor work to do, major work required

Garden

e.g. Small, medium, large

Garage

e.g. Single, double, none

Price per square foot*

Useful analysis data

* Calculating the price per square foot (see box, overleaf) of a property is a useful analysis as sometimes a property can feel 'huge' versus another one with more, but smaller, rooms. It also helps to work out how much extra you pay for a better area, or having a garage and larger garden. Furthermore, it highlights how a potential buyer might assess your home versus others for sale in the area and, of course, you could use a similar table to compare the properties you are interested in buying.

Calculating the price per square foot

When you are making property comparisons (see page 87), use the property details or measure the rooms in your own home to calculate the price per square foot (or metre if you prefer).

Dining room	12 x 12ft = 144sq ft
Kitchen	12 x 8ft = 96sq ft
Bedroom	10 x 8ft = 80sq ft
Bathroom	6 x 4ft = 24sq ft
Total square foot	**344sq ft**

Divide the value by the total square foot of the property's rooms. For example, if the property is worth £100,000, divide by 344sq ft, which equals £290 per sq ft.

Over the course of buying or selling a property there are various prices that will be linked to yours. It is important not to get too 'attached' to one and refuse to negotiate: your home is only worth what someone else is willing to pay – and accept – for it. So don't forget that even though you have accepted or had an offer accepted, the price of a property isn't necessarily guaranteed. The only time it is guaranteed is when contracts are exchanged as at that stage no more negotiation can take place without one party having to forfeit costs to the other.

Case Study   Richard

During the course of a house sale, its price can vary and this case outlines a not unusual chain of events.

Richard put his house on the market at £199,000 (price 1). A buyer duly offered £190,000 for it (price 2), but Richard had decided that he would only drop as far as £195,000 so negotiated the price up to that figure (price 3).

In came the surveyor, who found some damp, but as he felt the buyer was getting a good deal at £195,000 he still valued the property at that level. But the mortgage valuer found the same damp and recommended that it would cost £1,000 to put right, so she only valued the property at £194,000 (price 4).

Last, but not least, Richard and his buyer then had to negotiate a final price and they decided to 'split the difference' and so the selling price was agreed at £194,500 (price 5).

Selling your home

An important decision to make when selling your home is which (if any) estate agent to use: a choice that could have a major impact on how you sell your property. There is also guidance on good selling practice, and how to deal with any problems at this stage. Sellers also have to be better prepared than ever before with the introduction of Home Information Packs, which are fully explained.

Getting yourself ready

If we sell our possessions, it's usually because we don't want or need them any more. If they have any emotional connotations, it is with the past. Selling your home is different: it is part of your present life, it is where you and your loved ones live, and (the point that can lead to major hold-ups later on) you probably bought it because you fell in love with it.

This emotional attachment to bricks and mortar is perfectly natural: the home shelters and protects us and is the setting for family life with all its ups and downs. At some level we can feel that by selling the home we are rejecting part of the family. This brings an emotional tinge to the selling process, which can be intensified by the reason for the sale. Separation, bereavement and retirement, for example, are major life events with related emotions yet are often the spur for a house sale, bringing a tangle of associations to a business transaction.

It is important that you recognise that you too are likely to have feelings about your property and that this can affect how you behave. Quite a lot of people take their property off the market at a late stage in proceedings because they suddenly realise they don't want to move after all. Someone who is harbouring such feelings is likely to be slow to deal with paperwork, unclear in their communication and generally hold things up in a subconscious bid to stop it happening at all.

> **❝ It is perfectly natural to have an attachment to bricks and mortar: our homes shelter and protect us and they are the setting for family life with all its ups and downs. ❞**

 Chapter 2 (see pages 23–72) gives you advice on working out how much you can afford (a vital part of the process), and Chapter 3 (see pages 73–88) includes information on valuing a property.

BE CLEAR ABOUT THE MONEY

Follow the information on how much you can afford in Chapter 2 (pages 23–72), and on property valuing in Chapter 3 (pages 73–88). This will help you set a maximum price that you would like to get for your house, and the minimum price that would still enable you to buy your next property. In the long journey ahead, keep both figures in mind, not just the maximum one: remember you are moving to live in a new home, not necessarily to make your fortune.

What will you sell?

Some fixtures and fittings are often included in the sale price. This includes curtains, carpets, door furniture and bathroom fittings, appliances, storage heaters and even sometimes the furniture itself. In every room, including the shed and the garage, decide what:

- You are definitely taking with you.
- You are prepared to negotiate over.
- You definitely don't want. You will have to dispose of these items if your buyer does not want them either. It may be easiest to get rid of them now: less clutter means more space, and space sells property.

❝ Decide on a potential minimum selling price that would mean you could still afford to buy your next property. ❞

Think through whether you would want to sell anything that neither you nor your buyer wants. If you have bulky, unwanted items that you can't transport, your local council may be prepared to remove them for you for a small charge.

Write down the items, by room, for each category. Your estate agent and, later, your solicitor will need this information.

Jargon buster

Joint tenancy When two people own a property together and if one dies it automatically passes to the other, irrespective of the will
GCH Abbreviation for gas central heating

Get the paperwork ready

You will be asked to provide various items of paperwork at some stage. Get it all ready in advance and there won't be a big panic or delay when you have to find it. You will need:

- **The buying information** you were given when you purchased your house. Much of the information won't have changed (unless you have extended it or changed the layout, altering the room sizes). ✓

- **Any building regulations certificates** or planning permission information given if you have extended the property or it was extended before. ✓

- **Electrical certificates** if you have had re-wiring done since January 2005. Once Improvement Packs are in place, these will need to be shown or you'll need to get in an inspector. ✓

- **Any other documentation** that you have from when you purchased your property. ✓

- **Current bills** for council tax and supplies such as gas, electricity and water. This will allow you to demonstrate the running costs of the home. ✓

- **Buildings insurance,** again for reference and because you will need to change this policy to your new property. ✓

- **Contents insurance,** for the same reason. ✓

- **Mortgage roll/account number.** You'll need this later, but some sales have been held up for weeks as the seller tries to track it down. ✓

- **After June 2007,** you will need to prepare a Home Information Pack before putting your house on the market (see pages 105–8). ✓

Estate agents

Estate agents as a whole have a poor reputation in the UK. One problem is that anyone can set up as one (they don't have to pass exams or get a licence), and there are certainly some rogue estate agents carrying out some sharp practice around. Fortunately, there are also plenty of experienced operators who provide an excellent professional service, so the critical task is to find a good one.

If you sell your own house, you will save a substantial sum (the typical estate agent's fee is between 1.5 and 2 per cent, which pays £2,250–£3,000 on a £150,000 property). The drawback is the time and work that you will have to put in yourself. If you try but fail to sell your house, you won't save anything, but you still lose the time and the opportunity to move. For more information, see pages 103–4.

WHAT DOES AN ESTATE AGENT DO?

A good estate agent will visit your property and suggest three possible prices (see page 97, which includes other advice on what to ask them at this stage). Once you have chosen an agent and the price you want to put it on the market for, the agent should:

- **Send you a contract** (see page 100) setting out their terms and conditions.
- **Measure and photograph** the property to produce the sales particulars, checking them through with you.
- **Help you to get your Home Information Pack** when they come in (see pages 105–8), if you want them to. There will be other providers, too.
- **Put a 'For sale' board** outside your property (assuming you want one; your estate agent should give you the option).
- **Advertise your property** locally (and possibly nationally or in other regions such as London – it's important to negotiate this as it doesn't always happen automatically).

 The three suggested asking prices that an estate agent will give you will be the asking price, a fair price and a lower price. For more information on this and how to make your decision for which price to go for, see pages 97–8.

- **Advertise it at their premises** and via their website as well as directly to a list of potential buyers.
- **Arrange viewings** for legitimate potential buyers (and show people around your house if you aren't there).
- **Receive offers,** communicating them to you in writing and negotiating on your behalf.
- **Liaise** between your buyer, you and your solicitor.
- **Arrange** the handover of keys on completion day.

You could do most of this yourself. However, there are various benefits a good agent brings.

❝In any field, experience is valued. Selling is a skill as is dealing with problems.❞

Property surveyors

Some estate agency practices are run by property surveyors and they tend to have a good feel of the overall market as they will be members of **RICS** and are likely to contribute to and receive their **property price surveys** (see pages 75-9). They also survey other properties locally, so tend to have a wider knowledge of individual local property prices.

Experience

In any field, experience is valued. Someone who has spent years helping people buy and sell property should be able to forestall problems, keep the process moving efficiently and effectively, and offer informed advice when decisions are required.

Marketing

Selling is a skill. No one is going to persuade an unwilling buyer to purchase your property, but a professional sales person will be able to communicate effectively, pointing out advantages and answering queries that might otherwise have put someone off. In addition, a good agent will have the resources to market your property nationally via their website.

Security

Inviting strangers into your home carries a risk. You don't know who they are and you can't vet them, but you could find yourself alone with them in your home. Sadly, these days this is not wise. An agent who accompanies viewers means that you won't be put in a vulnerable position.

Avoiding time-wasters

You can never be sure if a viewer is genuinely interested in your property, and some people seem to make a hobby of looking around houses that are on the market when they have no intention of buying. A good agent will check if the buyer is serious and ask if they have a Mortgage Agreement in

Principle (see page 40). If they haven't arranged a loan (which means there's no guarantee they can afford to buy your home), the agent can set this in motion.

Accessibility

Any decent agent will have someone available to talk to potential buyers. You might not be able to do this.

Jargon buster

Break clause The point at which a sole agency can be terminated (see page 100)

Mortgage Agreement in Principle An expression of a mortgage lender's willingness to enter into an agreement subject to other conditions being met. Also known as an MAP

Property portal Website with properties from a variety of agents

Property price surveys National surveys that study trends in the property market (see pages 75-9)

RICS Royal Institution of Chartered Surveyors

Surveyor Qualified person who assesses the structural soundness of your home

HOW TO GET THE BEST AGENT

When it comes to choosing an agent, read the advice on studying your local property market on pages 79–82. This should give you an idea of which agents are not just *marketing* properties like yours, but *selling* them. In a high street with six agents, only two or three may be right for you, so it is always advisable to do some preliminary research by asking local people for recommendations.

Also look at who is advertising properties like yours in the local paper and possibly on the internet. Estate agents tend to specialise and clearly there is absolutely no point asking one who usually sells large, expensive houses with land to market a small flat.

A common mistake when choosing an agent is the 'board count' method, which means a vendor goes for the agent with the most boards in the area. However, the agent with the most 'For sale' boards is not necessarily the most successful at selling your type of property – they may have a big push on to increase their market share, or be pulling in sellers (but not buyers) with misleadingly high prices.

 For news on the Which? Move It! campaign (see box at the top of the following page) go to www.which.net/moveit/index.html. On this site you will find current news and updates on proposals to regulate estate agents.

The Move it! campaign

Which? is campaigning for estate agents to be properly regulated so that they are licensed by an independent body. Which? also believes an effective, independent and mandatory ombudsman scheme is needed, so that when things go wrong, you can get justice without going to court and dishonest traders can be put out of business. Despite the poor reputation of estate agents, over 93 per cent of properties are sold through them. The key is to find the right agent for you: someone who behaves professionally, with experience in selling your type of property, with good knowledge of the local market, and who you feel comfortable with. A good agent will reduce the worry and workload of selling a property and, priced correctly, should be able to get you to an agreed sale within 8–12 weeks. A bad one can turn an always stressful process into a nightmare.

Location location

Just as the location of your house is important, so is the site of your estate agent. Your agent should be based in a town as near as possible to your property, and already be dealing in properties in your area. If your property is located between two towns, see which one has more agents who work in your area. If the split is equal, you may be better off using two agents (on a more expensive multiple agency deal – see page 100) because between them they will market your property more widely.

Check out where the agent's offices are. An upmarket location near a stylish clothes shop in the high street will attract different buyers to the one at the end of the street next to a scruffy pub or discount shop.

“ An estate agent based in an upmarket location in the busy high street will attract different buyers to the one based in a scruffy street on the edge of town. ”

Who is your buyer?

What type of person is most likely to buy your property? An upmarket childless couple? A family with young children? An older person who wants to be near the shops? Now consider which agents appeal to that sector. Look at where they place advertisements and their style. Huge colour photographs of palatial residences won't attract someone looking for a bedsit: they're busy studying the page with small black-and-white pictures of flats.

Get a valuation

Any decent estate agent will be willing to visit your house to make a free valuation. Invite three who have passed your initial checks described above to do this, asking them to bring details of any similar properties on the market or which they have sold in the last six months.

Go around the property with them, inviting comments on any factors that will be attractive or not to potential buyers. This may help you see your property with fresh eyes, seeing the good points and spotting flaws, such as damaged doors, cracked plaster or peeling paper.

Nothing structural

Remember that agents are not surveyors and will not be looking for, or be trained to identify, any structural faults in the property. If you know of any, tell them now: they should be mentioned in the Home Information Pack, and are anyway likely to be discovered by your buyer's **surveyor**, and could affect the outcome of your sale. Discuss with the agent whether you should:

- Have major repairs made before putting the house on the market.
- Get estimates in from builders so that you are equipped to negotiate from an informed standpoint.

A good estate agent will suggest three possible prices for you to consider:

- An asking price.
- A **fair price** if you cannot achieve the asking price.
- A **lower price** likely to sell the property within six weeks.

Ask them their reasons for choosing each price. They may mention minor repairs like cracked window panes that you can easily fix and which have a big impact on the feel of a place. They will also know how many people are looking for properties of this type, and that will certainly affect the asking price. Ask them how many properties they have had on the market in the last 12 weeks and how many of those have actually sold.

Going through this process with three agents will give you a good idea of the likely asking and final selling price. If the price range differs by more than 5 per cent, talk to a couple more agents.

Making your decision

Overleaf there are a suggested list of questions to ask your potential agents, which will help you narrow down your choice of which agent to go with.

When choosing your asking price, remember that just as £4.99 is a more attractive price than £5.00, so £149,950 seems a far more attractive price than £150,000.

Key questions to ask an estate agent

- How many similar properties have you sold? ✓
- What prices did they achieve? ✓
- How long did they take to sell? ✓
- How many viewings did it take to gain a sale? ✓
- How many buyers have you got looking in my price range? ✓
- When you mail out my details, how many will you mail out to? ✓
- Are any of your buyers in a cash or sold position? ✓
- Will you advertise my property all the time in your window? ✓
- Will you advertise my property in the local property newspaper every week? ✓
- Which property portals do you advertise on? (For example, do you use Rightmove or Fish4Homes?) ✓
- Who will deal with my property? (If possible, have a chat with that person.) ✓
- Will you only send viewers who already have their loan finance sorted out? ✓
- How might you deal with any problems (for examples, see pages 120-2)? (A good agent can help to keep the process moving smoothly.) ✓

Codes of practice

Sadly, estate agents are not regulated. However, trade associations they can belong to have codes of practice for their members, and will handle complaints if you are unhappy. Ask if your agent is a member of the Royal Institution of Chartered Surveyors (RICS) (www.rics.org), the National Association of Estate Agents (NAEA) (www.naea.co.uk) or the Ombudsman for Estate Agents (OEA) (www.oea.co.uk). If they say they are, contact that association and check: agents have been known to lie about this. If your estate agent is a member of the OEA, you have improved access to redress. If the OEA finds in your favour, you may be compensated.

- Are you a member of any association? ✓

- If not, why not? ✓

- What estate agency qualifications have you/your staff got? ✓

- Can I see a copy of your terms and conditions? ✓

- What if I want to market my property privately too? (You need a 'sole agency'; see page 100.) ✓

- What charges do you make apart from your agency fees? ✓

- If I give you sole agency, how long will I be locked into a contract? (It is best to have a break clause after six or eight weeks, when you can go to another agent if you wish.) ✓

- If you are not introducing buyers or getting offers, can I break the contract? ✓

- If I have a complaint, how is it handled? Are you a member of the Ombudsman for Estate Agents (see box, opposite)? ✓

- How many different members of staff will help buyers view the property? ✓

- Will you accompany buyers on all the viewings? ✓

- Do you do weekend and evening viewings? ✓

- What procedures do you have to follow up after a viewing? ✓

- How do you check that buyers can afford my property? ✓

- Are floor plans and pictures included in the property details? ✓

- Have you got a sales progression department that will chase the chain? ✓

THE CONTRACT

You can avoid many potential problems by reading the estate agent's contract, making sure you understand it and re-negotiating anything you don't like before you sign it.

Many disputes between sellers and agents stem from misunderstanding the contract. If you don't understand the contract, don't sign it: you may be better off with a different agent. Read the contract carefully and look for these terms.

Sole, joint or multiple agency

- A 'sole selling agent' will have the exclusive right to sell your property and will be paid, even if you find a buyer yourself. However, it is important to negotiate this beforehand in writing and check the terms as not every agent will do this.
- A 'sole agency' is still the only agent, but they don't get paid if you find a buyer.
- Both of these will cost less than **joint** (two) or **multiple agents**, who will charge a higher commission rate to compensate for the fact that only one of them will get paid. See page 96 for advice on when it can be worth having more than one agent.

The fee

Estate agents charge a percentage, plus VAT, of the final selling price. Rates vary, but are typically 1.75 per cent for sole agency, and 2–3.5 per cent for multiple or joint arrangements. These rates are negotiable, but remember the agent has been through this process many more times than you have. It is worth

 See the information on property price surveys in Chapter 3 (pages 73–88) to gain more of an idea of the potential value of your property. This will help you when choosing which estate agent you will go with.

Jargon buster

Completion The day when your house sale, purchase or remortgage is finalised

Exchange of contracts The process of making an agreement to buy and sell a house legally binding

Joint agency When you have two agents selling your property

Multiple agent When you have more than two agents selling your property

Sole agency One estate agent has the exclusive right to sell your property

Tie-in period The length of time when you are tied to a sole, joint or multiple agency

asking the estate agent how much in real terms the fee could be, this will help you budget more effectively.

Ready, willing and able purchaser

If the contract contains a term stating 'ready, willing and able purchaser', walk away – don't sign any contract with it. It will mean that you'll still have to pay the estate agent for finding you a buyer even if your situation changes and you have to withdraw from the sale.

Payment

Choose an agent that gives you a few days for the money to transfer before charging interest. And make sure it requires payment when the sale is **completed** rather than when contracts are **exchanged**. Do not hand over the authority to pay the estate agent to anyone else (known as irrevocable

 If the agent tries to charge a 'fixed fee', even if it is expressed as a percentage of the asking price (not the selling price): it means they'll bill you for that fee no matter what the property actually sells for. This is bad value if your price drops, but can be a good deal if the fee is set at a lower percentage of a highly priced property.

❝ Do not sign a contract that contains the term 'ready, willing and able purchaser'. ❞

 Websites for relevant trade associations are: www.naea.co.uk (National Association of Estate Agents), www.oea.co.uk (Ombudsman for Estate Agents) and www.rics.org.uk (Royal Institution of Chartered Surveyors).

If you know of someone that might be interested in your property, but still want to put it on the market with an agency, tell the agent (in writing) that you may have a private buyer before you sign the contract. If the private buyer, dealing direct with you, subsequently purchases your property, you will not be liable to pay the estate agent a fee.

buys your home within six months of a contract ending. But some agents go further and state that you have to pay this, no matter how long it is after the termination of a contract.

YOUR RIGHTS WHEN DEALING WITH AN AGENT

It's your legal right that estate agents must do the following:

- **Pass on all offers on a property.** There have been cases where offers have not been passed on to the vendor simply because a person making a lower offer has agreed to use the estate agent's mortgage services.
- **Pass on offers promptly** in writing. They shouldn't just telephone you to inform you of an offer.
- **Use clear contract terms.**
- **Reveal to you** any financial interest that they have in offers made on your property. For example, they are not allowed to collude with property developers so that the only offers they pass on to you are those that suit their interests.

authority – you should avoid this). If you have a complaint about the service provided, you won't have the power to withhold payment.

Tie-in periods

Avoid lengthy **tie-in periods** of anything over eight weeks. And remember to factor in the notice period, which is often two weeks – you can't usually give notice until the minimum contract period is over.

Open-ended agreements

Check what happens when the contract ends. Some agents operate a 'six-month rule' whereby you have to pay them if a buyer they introduced

If you suspect that an agent has acted in breach of these regulations, you should contact the local authority trading standards department together with the professional association, if they are a member.

Selling your property yourself

If your research into the local market reveals that demand for property of your type is high, and houses seem to be selling quickly, suggesting a buoyant market, why not try to sell it yourself? This is a particularly good idea if you already know someone who wants to buy it – a friend or contact, or perhaps someone who put a note through the letterbox asking if you were interested in selling.

If you sell your property yourself, you will certainly save a big chunk of money – but buyers will be aware of this and may try to negotiate a lower price to share in the saving. If your property has a complicated leasehold situation or if ownership is disputed, don't try selling it yourself.

How can you sell your own property?

About eight out of every ten property buyers are already local (within five miles), so you need to spread the word in your area. Tell your friends and contacts and put up a 'For sale' board (see box, right) – don't underestimate the power of the board.

You'll need to prepare sales particulars for potential buyers and to remind viewers of what your property was like. Although this information is not subject to the Property Misdescriptions Act (which applies to particulars prepared by estate agents), it must be accurate. It should include:

- **Interior and exterior** photographs.
- **A floor plan** if possible (often a major selling tool).
- **A general description** followed by room-by-room details (see box on page 104).
- **Details of what is included** in the sale (such as curtains and any appliances), the council tax band and cost, and the asking price and your contact details.

There are legal requirements about 'For sale' boards. You can only use one up to 0.5sq m, or two joined together to a maximum of 0.6sq m. They must have a different advertisement on each side. Remember also that they need to be securely positioned – you don't want them clobbering a potential buyer (or anyone else!).

103

Room by room

The description should include a concise room-by-room guide to the house, text for each room stating its size (in metres), the number of windows, telephone, radiators, electric and TV cable points and other points of interest, such as open fireplaces or fitted wardrobes. Imagine the route you will take to show buyers, and follow this room order in the particulars.

Look at the particulars on other properties from a range of estate agents to help you with the style and content of your own particulars.

You could place advertisements in the local press, but they are unlikely to attract the attention achieved by the large colour spreads of the agents. You can get a reasonable-sized advert for £150 or more. However, smaller local publications, such as parish newsletters, are a cost-effective possibility, as are advertising-only papers, such as *Loot* and *Dalton's Weekly*. Another route is private property sale websites, such as www.propertybroker.co.uk and www.propertyweb.co.uk. You could also create your own advertisement to place in newsagents and other local shops, companies and offices, and sports and social clubs – anywhere with a noticeboard where you're allowed to put up an advert.

ᏟᏟ If you sell your property yourself, you will save lots of money – but buyers will be aware of this and may try to negotiate a lower price to share in the saving. ᏓᏓ

What if you don't sell it?

If you don't sell your property or gain any interest within 8–12 weeks, you may need to swallow your pride and use an estate agent. It may be worth considering taking it off the market for a while first, before putting it back on sale through an agent.

 It is important that you prepare your home for sale so that it looks its best. See pages 114–18 for guidance. There is also information there on showing viewers around your home.

Home Information Packs

From 1 June 2007, anyone putting their property on the market in England and Wales will be legally required to prepare a Home Information Pack (HIP). There will be dry runs to check the system in advance of this. This is the biggest change in the law relating to buying and selling property in the last 100 years and requires knowledge of some fundamental changes.

HIPs will be introduced because more than 30 per cent of property transactions have been falling through between acceptance of the offer and exchange of contracts, at an estimated cost in wasted money of £350 million, or nearly £1 million a day, and with incalculable costs in terms of time and anxiety.

More than two-fifths of these failures were the result of survey or **valuation** inspection reports, which found faults with the property. When you consider that only one in five buyers bother with a full survey, it is clear that many buyers get a nasty surprise when they move into their new properties and discover an urgent need for repairs.

The HIP is designed to reduce the risk of this happening by making the whole process clearer: sellers and buyers will know more about the property they are negotiating over at an earlier stage. If the pack highlights a problem with the property, the seller can deal with it by getting estimates for work required and lowering their asking price to allow for it, avoiding the hassle of negotiation later on. The buyer will be able to make an

HIP point

Schemes similar to the HIP already run successfully in Denmark and Australia. The scheme was piloted in Bristol in 2000 and tried as a test run in some regions from June 2006. Which? actively campaigned for the introduction of HIPs and consumer surveys in England and Wales show massive public support.

 Most of the other failed sales collapse because buyers can't raise the right finance: a reminder of the importance of a Mortgage Agreement in Principle (see page 40) and making sure you can afford to buy what you view (see pages 33-5).

Jargon buster

Condition ratings Different levels of the property's condition, as laid down in the home condition report
Conveyancer Person who carries out the legal and administrative process involved in transferring the ownership of loan or any building from one owner to another
Home condition report Part of the HIP that contains essential information about the property (see right)
Listed building A building that has special preservation orders on it
Right of way A public path, track or road passing through your property
Valuation Lenders carry out a valuation before they agree to lend to you. The report gives a brief description of any problems that would affect the value of a house

Who will do the survey?

When HIPs first appear, there may not be enough surveyors in England and Wales to produce reports on properties likely to be offered for sale. It is estimated that 7,000 new, qualified home inspectors are needed to conduct well over a million surveys a year.

informed decision on whether and what to offer. So with so much information already in place, fewer sales will fall through, plus they should go through more smoothly and (once the property is on the market) faster. A HIP probably won't reduce the overall time taken to sell your house as it may take longer to set up the process, but as a result it should be quicker to exchange once you have received an offer.

How will it work?

Before you put your property up for sale, you will have to prepare the HIP or someone can do the HIP for you. You do not need one for a private sale in which you do not market your property, e.g. for agreeing a sale with your neighbour. The report is designed to be read and understood by a layman. It includes a **home condition report**, divided into sections, which are likely to include:

- **Section A** explains the terms of the report, including the **condition ratings** used later on (on a scale of 1–3) and what is and is not inspected.
- **Section B** gives a general briefing on the property: age, size, accommodation, re-building cost (useful for getting buildings insurance quotes) and general

 The home condition report (known as a level 2 survey) will contain slightly more information than the homebuyer survey, see page 153, known as level 1) and a full buildings survey (level 3, see also page 153).

construction, together with an overall opinion of the property and a summary of the condition ratings.

- **Section C** states whether the building is **listed** or has a **right of way** near or through it, planning consents, plus environmental and health and safety matters, such as flood risk. This provides a briefing for the **conveyancer** on what legal points will need to be followed up and is similar to the searches they currently do.
- **Section D** gives a detailed description of the exterior of the property, including chimneystacks, the roof, pipes and gutters, windows and doors.
- **Section E** looks at the condition of the interior, including roof space, walls and floors, fireplaces, chimneys.
- **Section F** deals with the electricity, gas, water, heating and drainage services.
- **Section G** covers permanent outbuildings (so not garden sheds), grounds and boundaries.
- **Section H** is a report on the property's energy efficiency.

The rest of the HIP is likely to include this material, previously organised solely by a conveyancer (for more information see pages 110–11). After the introduction of the HIPs, most of these items will not be compulsory and although a fixtures and fittings list will be included in the pack, there will be no obligation for the home owner to fill it in:

- Legal pack
- Home use and home contents forms
- Fixtures and fittings list
- Legal summary
- Terms of sale
- Evidence of title
- Answers to standard preliminary enquiries by buyers
- Copies of planning, listed building and building regulations consents and applications
- For new properties, copies of warranties and guarantees
- Replies to local authority, water and drainage searches.

Leasehold property reports are also likely to contain:

- Memorandum and articles of association of the management company, plus a copy of their company accounts
- Buildings insurance information (an up-to-date schedule of the policy outlining what parts of the building it is responsible for and how much it will cost the purchaser)
- Copies of any previous planning consents and buildings regulations
- Copy of the lease
- Copy of a receipt for rent and service charge, if available.

What will it cost?

The charge for producing a HIP is likely to be around £600, of which half is the cost of the home condition report. However, conveyancing fees should fall as the HIP covers much of what a conveyancer does (see pages 110–13). Also, most of the items in the pack will have to be bought at some stage anyway, so the £600 is not all new, extra cost. In addition, it is very likely that some agents or legal companies will offer HIPs on a 'no move, no fee' basis. There is certainly a shift in costs from the buyer to the seller, but since most sellers are also going to purchase another property, this balances out. It is likely that big banks and other companies will enter into the market, so consumers should shop around for a HIP.

 Much of the information in the HIP will remain valid for decades, but the condition of the property is likely to change over time, and local searches are only valid for three months. If a property is on the market for a long time, some parts of the HIP may need updating.

Who will provide it?

The introduction of HIPs marks an opportunity for estate agents, lenders, legal firms and surveyors to build their presence in the property market by offering the packs as part of their service. The HIP may become an incentive tool that will encourage you to select a certain agent, lender or legal firm.

It is difficult to say in advance which sector will find the best way to do it, but the market has a way of producing what is needed. In time, many firms will be proudly offering Home Information Packs as part of their portfolio, even though many bitterly resisted the change when it was first suggested.

“It is difficult to say in advance which sector will find the best way to provide a HIP, but the market has a way of producing what is needed.”

The legal process

The legal aspect of your house sale must be carried out to the letter, or the whole process could fall through. Don't leave finding a conveyancer until you have a buyer: sort it out in advance, thereby saving time and hassle. Conveyancing usually takes about two months, but this may fall after the introduction of HIPs.

Paperwork delays can significantly hold up the selling process. Make sure that you read everything you are sent, and deal with it as quickly as possible, returning it by hand or registered post. If there's anything you don't understand, pick up the phone or email your legal company.

CHOOSE A LEGAL FIRM

You need to use either a solicitor or a licensed conveyancer. All solicitors are qualified to do this work, but it is a specialist job so make sure whoever you go to is experienced in this field. Costs vary widely, and there are some very good internet-based providers, such as www.easier2move.co.uk and www.legalmove.com. Internet providers will mainly have a solicitor panel they will give your work to. They will give you access to your case over the internet and text you updates and you can deal with the solicitor allocated in whatever way you wish, many of which operate on fixed fees. A no completion, no fee service is also offered. Most of the information comes via email, so your conveyancer doesn't have to be local (although it might save time on occasion, and you might feel more confident you can keep things moving if they are on your doorstep). Check out the following:

- **The firm or department** specialises in conveyancing.
- **The person handling your work** isn't due to go on holiday or, if they are, who will cover for them.
- **They know your preferred exchange and completion date** and can work to it. Some conveyancers handle hundreds of cases at a time so make sure they have a limit to the number they choose – it should be no more than 100 and you want to be on the top of their pile.
- **Ask about charges.** These vary a lot. The cheapest may not be the best. See also the 'seven questions' initiative, which offers advice on choosing a legal firm: www.consumerdirect.gov.uk.

❝To save time, draw up a draft contract ahead of a sale.❞

Instruct your legal firm

You will need to 'instruct' a legal company to carry out your conveyancing as soon as you have agreed an offer on your home – so it makes sense to find one that you are happy with ahead of this. As long as you are sure you are going to sell your home, choose your conveyancer as soon as you put your house on the market. In this way you can give your solicitor time to prepare contracts and get the necessary details from you. When a buyer is found, all contract documentation can be sent immediately.

They will require proof of identity, such as a passport or birth certificate, a marriage certificate if the property is jointly owned, plus proof of your address, such as a recent utility bill. Once they have this, they will also need your estate agent's details and your mortgage roll/account number. They can ask for the **deeds** from the lender (unless you already have them) and draw up a draft contract (unless you have one in your Home Information Pack). Getting this organised ahead of a sale can save six weeks delay further down the line.

Fill in the property information and fixtures and fittings forms

Until the implementation of the Home Information Packs, you will be sent a questionnaire by your conveyancer requiring information on:

- Your mortgage
- Who owns the various boundaries of the property
- Any disputes with neighbours
- The mains services available
- Copies of any guarantees (such as for damp courses, wiring, plumbing or timber treatment) or planning permission and details of any building work done.

There will also be a form setting out the fixtures and fittings that are included in the sale. You may not yet know which of these are included, so confirm what you can and mark the rest 'TBC' for 'to be confirmed'. This information will be part of the HIP (see pages 105–17).

AFTER AN OFFER IS AGREED

Once you have accepted an offer, your representative will contact your buyer's solicitor to check on where they are in their house sale and obtaining a mortgage. Tell your

Do it yourself?

You can do your own conveyancing but there's less incentive these days as the introduction of specialist firms has cut fees. You can buy the documents from a legal stationer and fill them in yourself, then apply to the Land Registry for the other documentation needed. It's time-consuming, calls for a good eye for detail and mistakes could land you in court.

On the other hand, you'll know everything that's going on and the reason for any delays and you'll save on fees and mark-ups on costs. Conveyancing for new houses or flats is more complicated than for other property types. You can pay a solicitor to check your paperwork once you have done it – they'll charge around £100 for this. Some mortgage lenders will not accept you purchasing a property (with their money!) without a legal representative.

Go for no sale, no fee and fixed fee

Busy conveyancers with too many cases on their desk are forced into a 'fire fighting' approach: they pick up a file that's due to exchange, realise something is missing, request it, and won't chase it for a week. Delays can lead to failed contracts. 'No sale, no fee' deals give them an incentive to get the job done quickly because it reduces the

chances of hold-ups and they are more likely to get paid for finishing the job. Most 'no sale, no fee' firms also offer 'fixed-fee' conveyancing, which means you only pay the price you sign up to, so the more efficient they are, the more likely they are to make a profit. This is potentially the opposite for those that charge by the hour!

solicitor of any conditions of the sale, such as an agreed time to complete, and supply dates for when you want to exchange and complete.

Read and sign the contracts

Your legal company should draw up your contract of sale within a matter of weeks of you instructing them. Ask for this and read it carefully before signing. It will be in two parts:

- **The particulars of sale,** which describe the property and give the terms of the lease or freehold.
- **The conditions of sale,** which include the proposed completion date and what deposit is required on exchange of contracts.

Your legal firm will send an identical contract to the buyer's solicitor with copies of the title deeds.

Answer your buyer's questions

Often at this stage the buyer's representative will have questions about your property. Answer these as quickly as you can. This is frequently the biggest cause of delay for exchange. It is what the conveyancer forgets to 'ask for' in advance, or what the buyer's legal company forgets to answer. Some companies have standard questions they send out, which can be done automatically. You should ensure that you put in writing any questions you need answered

about the property and ensure your legal representative asks them well in advance of exchange.

Agree the deposit

Deposits from the buyer used to be straightforward. If you bought a property for less than £100,000, then you would pay 5 per cent at the time of exchange and for £100,000+ a 10 per cent deposit. However, with the massive property price rises from early 2000, many purchasers just don't have the cash to pay the 10 per cent, so some legal companies are accepting a 5 per cent cash deposit at time of exchange.

Exchange contracts

Once the contracts are signed and the deposit is paid, the legal companies phone all interested parties to confirm. Both parties are now legally committed to the purchase. A completion date will be set, usually for two weeks' time, but it can be sooner. This is a good time to check that you don't owe any money to the mortgage lender or the loan

 If you are only paying a 5 per cent deposit on a £100,000+ property and the sale falls through after exchange and doesn't complete, you are still likely to have to pay the full 10 per cent deposit.

company who lent you money based on your property, if you are selling for less than the money you owe.

Reach completion

The final balance to make the purchase is paid to your solicitor on completion day. If you are part of a chain, all these payments will be made one after the other.

Re-register title deeds

Your legal company can help you register the change of ownership within five weeks of completion at which point you pay the stamp duty.

As soon as (and never before) you hear that the money has been paid in, you can hand over the keys. To avoid a potentially embarrassing conversation on your doorstep where you (rightly) refuse to hand over the keys to the buyer, leave them with the estate agent, who will then not release them without your or the legal company's say-so.

Case Study Mr and Mrs Cooper

Always ask for proof at the outset that someone can afford to purchase your property. Mr and Mrs Cooper put their home up for sale in a small town by the sea. They were looking to move to a larger property so their children could have more room, and they both needed office space.

They put their home up for sale in February and gained an offer within the first two weeks, having sensibly priced the property and placed it with a well-known local agent. Sadly, the sale didn't proceed far after offers were confirmed and, after some more weeks,

the buyers pulled out – without giving any reason.

Sensibly, they had kept the property on the market and soon another buyer was found, this time a cash buyer, or so they said! Only a few weeks later, it turned out they couldn't raise the funds for the property. A few months later a third 'cash' buyer turned up but, again, the vendors were out of luck. It turned out that the latest buyers couldn't sell their holiday let.

At this stage, Mr and Mrs Cooper nearly gave up, but had found a property to buy with a very understanding couple.

So Mr and Mrs Cooper accepted this third 'cash' buyer but kept their house on the market just in case they could find yet another buyer. Surely not? But yes, another offer came through and this couple wanted to move fast, within a few weeks!

This time the vendors asked for a Mortgage Agreement In Principle and the purchasers had their solicitors already lined up. Exchange was eventually reached. So, don't forget – get that proof; lack of funding is the biggest reason for sales falling through after offers are made.

Selling your home

Most people selling and buying at the same time tend to concentrate on buying, whereas what you should be doing is looking at your home as if you were a potential buyer. For example, start with looking at it from the outside – how does it look?

Increasingly, potential buyers drive around an area and check out properties that are on the market before they make an appointment to view. So, look at your home with a view to:

- Is it tidy?
- **Does anything need repairing** that makes the property look uncared for? What about those little jobs like fixing an outside dripping tap or painting the windows?
- **Are the windows clean?**
- **Does the front door** look smart? (First impressions are crucial.)
- **Does the front garden** look cared for? Does the grass need a cut?

❝ Try to look at your home as though you were a buyer. ❞

PREPARING YOUR HOME

Inside, tour your home with fresh eyes. Walking around it with an estate agent when they are valuing can help here. Ask them if there is anything you need to improve, and follow their gaze to see where it falls. There are other things you can do to show your home in its best light to a buyer.

Know your buyer

If your property is likely to appeal to a first-time buyer, you could include appliances, curtains and carpets in the asking price as this will make it more attractive. If your target buyer is a family with young children, make it clear where pushchairs can be stored, and if you haven't got play equipment in the garden, put some in so it looks like a friendly space. If yours is a two-bedroom house with a box room suitable as a nursery, put a cot or small bed in it to show it fits.

 In addition to the other checks for estate agents (see pages 98–9), ensure the particulars about your property are accurate. Sometimes confusion has arisen because the property may need re-decorating but be presented on the particulars as requiring modernising, implying more work is required than is the case.

Tone it down

Buyers need to be able to picture themselves living in your home. This is much easier to do when the setting is neutral and uncluttered. If your walls are a bright pink, paint them a softer colour, however much it offends you. Strong colours put buyers off unless by some miracle they share your taste. Also get rid of any mould, grease, grime or limescale in bathrooms and kitchens.

Make a feature

Every room can benefit from having a memorable feature that makes it seem different to the rest. This could be a stained glass window or a lovely fireplace. If there isn't one, add a vase of flowers or a similarly striking accessory.

Create space

Buyers like to see large, airy, spaces: it's easier for them to imagine where their furniture will go. So use this as a good opportunity to clear out furniture or fittings that you no longer need. It will also save you money when you are booking or organising your removals.

Keep it tidy

Clutter puts buyers off. So get as many of your possessions as possible out of the way, into storage, the roof space or cupboards. Keep on top of the washing-up, too, so that a buyer isn't faced with a pile of dirty pans in the sink.

Be positive

However desperate you are to sell, and whatever reservations you may have about your property, smile and find positive things to say about it: the atmosphere you create will influence how people feel about your home.

❝Emphasise your home's strong points rather than the bad.❞

ARRANGING VIEWINGS

Your agent will arrange viewings. You will usually have at least a few hours', and possibly days', notice, but sometimes you'll get a phone call asking if they can pop around in a few minutes because it suits the buyer's

Take precautions

Don't show the property to viewers on your own unless you have some kind of proof of their identity, such as a landline number or address. In fact, if there is no agent present when showing a viewer around, ask a friend or relative to be present. Make sure someone else knows you have an appointment and who it is with. Keep valuables out of sight.

If you are arranging viewings yourself, get a landline phone number and ring them back to make the appointment (you can say you need to check timings with your partner).

schedule. Try to be gracious about this: you don't know which viewing is going to lead to a sale.

Some people prefer to let the agent show buyers round. Others feel they will do a better job of pointing out the good features of their own home themselves. You might end up showing people around at weekends, but leaving weekday appointments while you are at work to the agent.

Most properties look their best in daylight. Avoid mealtimes as buyers will feel uncomfortable watching the rest of your family eat, and will shorten their visit. Also, cooking smells can put people off.

If you do find it difficult to keep everything clean and tidy, then ask your estate agent about an 'open day'. It's something that is done often in Australia and can be quite effective. Basically the 'open day' is advertised and times given, then a series of bookings are made by the agent at, say, half-hourly intervals. The upside is that it makes it much easier for you, the slight downside is that it restricts when buyers can come. However, having an 'open day' does give a key 'date' for people to view your property and may help gain a sale, or even competitive bids.

WHAT TO SAY AND DO

Before showing anyone around, think of things you like about each part of your home. Some ideas are:

- **Exterior:** Convenient parking, helpful neighbours, a well-planted garden.
- **Kitchen/utility:** The lovely view from the kitchen window where you can watch the children playing in the garden, a good spot to leave dirty boots.
- **Living room:** The way you can dim the lights to change the mood, the high ceiling that gives a sense of space, or the low beams that add character and cosiness, the view it offers of the sunset.
- **Bedrooms:** The fact that they can take a double bed, the fitted wardrobes, the morning sunlight, the convenient en suite.
- **Bathrooms:** The elegant taps, the generously sized mirror, the sense of space.

 Agents usually ask for a set of keys so they can carry out viewings when you are out. You may also need to tell them how any alarm system works. If this is the case and you can't be in for viewings, ask for a copy of their key-handling policy. Some agents do not have a good security system for keys, and there have been cases of burglaries where keys left with estate agents have been used to enter properties and steal from them.

These show your home's advantages over similar properties. It is worth trying to work them into the conversation (not reciting them from a clipboard) and it gives you something to say other than, 'This is the lounge.' Type or write out the top ten points and give them to your agent so they can refer to them when they are conducting viewings.

People expect to come in through the main entrance, so even if you usually come in through the back door, welcome them at the front. If they have not got a set of sale particulars, offer them one, with a pen to make notes. It is usually best to start the tour in the living room. Complete the rest of the downstairs

area before moving upstairs. Then go out into the garden (have a couple of umbrellas handy in case of rain). At the end of the tour, ask if they felt what they have seen matched the particulars, and how they have found dealing with the agent. This allows them to give you information, which may help you market your property better, and you'll probably get an impression of how they feel about your home, too.

Information to keep and give out

This is something many sellers don't do, but it all helps.

- **Have copies** of the particulars of sale for reference.
- **Have a copy** of the Home Information Pack (see pages 105-7).
- **Keep examples of recent bills** (cross out confidential details such as account numbers) so that you can show running costs.
- **Have a copy of the local paper** as it helps give an impression of the area to outsiders.
- **Create a list of local** doctors, dentists, parks, playgroups, primary and secondary schools, libraries and anything else you think is uesful (gear it to your potential buyer).

First impressions

First impressions count. Buyers make decisions about whether they are interested in a property within seconds of their arrival. Making them feel comfortable makes it more likely they will view it in a positive frame of mind. Be polite, even if this is a surprise viewing that is delaying your shopping trip. Try not to appear over desperate to sell: it suggests either a problem, or an opportunity to negotiate the price down.

 A part of your agent's job (see page 99) is to telephone buyers a few days after the viewing to ask what they thought of it and if they have any questions or would like to view again. Feedback is useful as it will help you achieve a sale by changing things that put buyers off.

- **The nearest** leisure and shopping centres.
- **Menus of local restaurants** and takeaways give a feel for the locality and highlight convenience or exclusivity.
- **Local bus and train timetables** will be valuable to commuters or those who don't drive.

VETTING A BUYER AND THEIR OFFER

If someone makes an offer, there are a number of things to consider apart from the money.

- **Are they are a first-time buyer?** If so, your chain might be quite short (depending on who you are buying from), which is a big advantage.
- **When do they want to exchange** and complete? They may have a job-related deadline and so be, or not be, in a hurry.
- **Are they a couple who are separating?** This may complicate the selling process as people with possibly different priorities are involved.
- **Is their offer subject to a survey,** or are they happy with the information from the Home Information Pack? Not having another survey will shorten the process.

This information will help you decide what to do. Your estate agent should be able to offer advice here, but remember, although you are paying them, they only get paid if the property sells, so beware being pushed into selling low just for an early sale.

If the offer is below the asking price, the buyer should give reasons for this, and you can decide if they are valid. Remember your property is only worth what someone is prepared to pay for it. Bear in mind also that the market changes and your property might have risen or fallen in desirability in the last couple of months – check this out with your estate agent.

Once you accept an offer, the buyer might ask you to take the house off the market to avoid being gazumped. This is fair enough, but agree a date (for example, in two to six weeks) when you would return to the market if the sale hasn't progressed and/or you have not exchanged. Make sure that they can definitely afford your property and have already accepted an offer or sold their own.

Whatever the market conditions, communication is crucial. Don't disappear on holiday without telling everybody who needs to know. Respond to emails, letters and phone calls promptly and query anything you don't understand. Agree the timing of regular updates with your estate agent and legal firm.

Selling in different markets

SELLING IN A STRONG MARKET

You'll know from your research and conversations with estate agents and buyers if the market is buoyant with prices rising and properties selling quickly. You'll benefit from getting a good price on your property, but of course your purchase price may also be high. A rising market is fast moving, which adds to the stress of the whole process and means you need to turn around information quickly – so make sure you have all your paperwork and finances in place.

- Ensure you choose a buyer who is similarly well prepared, and negotiate an early completion date.

- You should aim to buy and sell at the same time in such a market to avoid losing touch with properties of the type you want to buy.

- With demand high it should be easier to sell a property with a drawback, like being on a main road, near a noisy pub or railway, but don't hesitate or try holding out for a higher price. If the market drops, you will be the first casualty.

SELLING IN A FALLING MARKET

If the price of your property is falling, it is likely to be the same with those that you are looking to buy, and you can actually benefit. For example, if you have to drop £5,000 on your sale price, but negotiate a £10,000 drop on your purchase, you gain £5,000.

- With falling prices there is a risk your buyer may try to renegotiate the price down later on, so agree an early deadline for exchange and completion to give them less time and opportunity.

- Patience is important in a slow market: accept that it will take longer to sell, and watch as more properties fall into your price range.

- The ideal scenario is to sell before buying, perhaps renting for six months then entering the market as one of those sought-after cash buyers.

Problems with your sale

The property selling system varies in different parts of the UK and Ireland, but wherever you are selling (and/or buying) there is enormous potential for problems. However, you can do a lot to avoid hitches by planning and proceeding sensibly and by taking advice along the way. Your sale is most certainly not as 'safe as houses' – 28 per cent of sales fall through after offer stage, with ramifications in many lives. Here are some ideas of what to do with specific problems.

NO VIEWINGS

Ask your agent how many sets of particulars of sale they have sent out and why they think no one is viewing. Perhaps you need to change some of the photographs or add floorplans, which can be more useful than photographs, because buyers can then see how the property could meet their needs.

Review your marketing strategy. You are either not reaching potential buyers (try different advertising media) or not impressing them. If the particulars of sale are okay, is the problem that your estate agent has a lack of buyers on their lists or it's a terrible market?

YOUR PROPERTY DOESN'T SELL

If your property does not sell within eight weeks, there is probably a problem with the valuation or the marketing, which includes the condition your home is in when people view it. If you think it's the latter, look again at pages 114–15. If you're concerned about lack of marketing, you could also try phoning the estate agent pretending to be a potential buyer in the area (or get a friend to do it), and see if they mention your property.

Review your asking price. Have prices dropped locally? What are similar properties selling for? Does your agent think a drop of £5,000 would stimulate new interest?

 Continue to bear in mind that clutter and untidiness around the home is not conducive to a quick sale. Look at pages 114-15 to remind you of what makes a home more attractive to a potential buyer.

One criticism levelled at estate agents is that as their commission (see page 93) is a fairly small percentage of the selling price, there is no incentive for them to push for a higher price, but plenty of incentive to get you to accept a lower amount as it makes little difference to the fee they will make. However, they don't get paid until your home sells, so there is still a large incentive.

BAD SURVEY

If your buyer's survey says there are problems with your property, ask for a copy of the relevant parts of the survey. Read it carefully: it may be pointing out potential rather than actual problems that require immediate attention. If you agree a repair is needed, get three estimates. Then you can choose whether to pay to get it done yourself or deduct the money from the sale price. Someone who has got as far as having a survey done has shown they like your property. They won't want to pull out. Incidentally, it is well worth tidying up before the surveyor arrives: part of their job is subjective and a tidy house is more attractive than one where there are piles of washing and toys.

BUYER WITHDRAWS

If this happens, you need to find out the reason why. They may have been refused a mortgage and be too embarrassed to tell anyone. However, other lenders may be willing to make them a loan: your agent or even your financial adviser should have some ideas on this. If they say they've gone off your property, ask why: even if this sale falls through, you're better equipped for the next one.

❝ If you agree a repair is needed to your home, get hold of three estimates. ❞

YOUR BUYER IS UNABLE TO FUND THE PURCHASE

This is a quite a common problem but should be avoidable if your estate agent is doing their job properly. Before accepting an offer, ask your agent to check with the purchaser that they have a Mortgage Agreement in Principle in place. If not, keep your property on the market until this is the case.

There can be a problem if the buyer decides to arrange their mortgage through the selling estate agent. This creates a conflict of interest as the agent is making money from both parties in the transaction and cannot therefore act in both their interests. For example, if it emerges that there is a problem with the potential purchaser affording the price they have offered, your estate agent might be tempted to try to lower the price rather than lose the sale and the mortgage arrangement fee. However, this may well happen even if the buyer has the same problem with a separate mortgage company and the agent doesn't want to lose the sale of the property either.

PROGRESS ON THE SALE IS VERY SLOW

Some buyers seem to view an offer as an 'option to buy' rather than a commitment to purchase, and about one in three purchases fall through. The key here is communication, asking the agent to check that the buyer is serious and has the finances in place before you take your property off the market. The average chain has seven houses. It only takes one sale to run into problems and the whole process grinds to a halt. A good agent will communicate up and down the chain and alert you to any problems.

❝ The average chain has seven houses. It only takes one sale to run into problems and the whole process grinds to a halt. ❞

CONTRACTS NOT EXCHANGED

Talk to your conveyancer and find out what is causing the delay. If you discover the buyer is holding things up or can't raise the finance, set a deadline after which you will put the property back on the market. Don't rely on the ordinary post: use registered post, a courier or deliver things by hand. Find out if there is a delay in another part of the chain and ask your agent or conveyancer to try to speed things up.

YOU FALL OUT WITH YOUR ESTATE AGENT

If you decide you want to withdraw instructions from your estate agent, inform them by phone first, making a note of the date and time of call and who you spoke to, and telling them you will confirm the conversation in writing. Your contract will tell you what notice period you have to give. Remember that if you instruct another agent during that period and they sell the house, you may still owe commission to your first agent – and you could have to pay double. So it makes sense to wait before appointing another agent, although you can still sell privately during this period as long as you didn't sign a contract that contained sole selling rights. Avoid this clause (see also page 100).

 Put all instructions and agreements in writing, and send them by registered post so that there can be no dispute on whether they arrived.

 If you should hit problems with your sale, see the box Codes of practice on page 98, which contains details of how estate agents are regulated and who you can contact if you need support.

Buying a property

The key to buying property is to understand your own needs so that you view places that match your way of life. This chapter discusses the different types of property, including new build, and explains how to check the location will suit you. Then it's on to searching for, viewing and checking out properties: our guidance should save you time and steer you towards the right home for you.

Needs versus wants

Buying a house is a major decision with huge implications for your life and your finances. However, many people do not approach it rationally, and it becomes a decision based on what they aspire to rather than what is right for them at this stage in their life. So start assessing what you do want by first choosing the property type that your prefer.

When you are briefing an agent, it is all too easy to describe your dream home rather than what you really need and then it can be a big let-down when you find you are not going to be able to have this ideal property. So, it is important to be as realistic as possible.

One in three offers falls through and the most common reason is that the buyer finds they can't afford the

> **❝ Be realistic and set an accurate brief that won't lead to frustration and change. ❞**

property that in an ideal world they'd really like. Around 25 per cent of buyers change their mind about what they want once they start looking at properties. That adds up to a lot of wasted time and effort all round. The key is to be realistic, to understand the implications of what you are asking for (every feature comes at a price) and to set an accurate brief that won't lead to frustration and change.

CHOOSING A PROPERTY TYPE

Here are three steps to deciding what property type you need and how to achieve it.

Step one

Imagine that you are going to buy a home, and make a list of the features you would look for. For many people, the list may include features such as a double garage, a spare room for guests, a hot tub, en suite with every bedroom, a playroom and a study.

This is your wants list.

Step two

Now imagine you are renting somewhere for a while, and write down what you really need. This list might include the following:

- A bedroom for each child.
- A living area big enough for your furniture.
- A garage or adequate private parking.
- A private, secure garden where your dog can exercise.

- A shared bathroom conveniently situated between two or three bedrooms.
- More storage space.
- Potential to extend.

This is your needs list.

Step three

The third stage is to look at what properties in your price bracket have to offer, and how they could be adapted to meet your needs and maybe a few of your wants. For example, a wooden cabin in the garden could function as a study or playroom. You may be able to fit in a bedroom for each child if some of them are single rather than double rooms.

Also consider the implications of the needs and wants list for the type of property you should look at.

- **Basic type:** house, bungalow, flat, mobile home.
- **Kind of house:** detached, semi-detached, terraced.
- **Kind of flat:** ground floor, first or top floor, penthouse, converted or purpose-built.
- **Bedrooms:** how many you need, and how many must be double.
- **Bathrooms/toilets:** how many you need.
- **What other rooms you need:** study, lounge, kitchen/diner, separate dining room.
- **Garden:** small, medium, large, with lawn, general condition.
- **Parking requirements:** off-street, in a garage or carport, for how many cars.

Spare room or hotel suite?

It's lovely to be able to offer guests their own space. But spare rooms are rarely used and often become dumping grounds for possessions on their way somewhere else in the home. If you calculate the extra cost of this largely unused spare room as part of your mortgage, you may find it far cheaper to do without and use the saved cash to book guests into a nearby hotel room as a base for when they come to stay.

CONSIDER DIFFERENT TYPES OF PROPERTY

With your list of needs and wants as a brief, you can now consider which type or types of property are best suited to meet it. Keep your mind open to all possibilities at this stage: you may have pictured yourself living in a Victorian cottage when, in fact, a new-build modern home ticks more of the boxes on your list.

Fashion victim?

Style magazines have a lot to answer for. It's surprising how fashion conscious the property market can be, and people can be led into choosing property styles that just don't suit them. One example is open-plan living/cooking areas. Some buyers realised after a while that they didn't like having cooking smells and sounds competing with the television or the book they were reading. Another example is the Industrial-style stainless-steel kitchens, which photograph beautifully but make some people feel as if they are in a factory.

Advantages and disadvantages of different styles of property

Age of property	Advantages	Possible drawbacks	Points to note
New homes	• Little maintenance required for first few years • Well-equipped and planned • Parking often planned in • Well insulated	• Rooms can be small • Gardens tend to be small • Can lack character • Tend to have 'thinner' walls, so not always good sound insulation	• People often think you don't need a proper survey on a new home, however you do • At least cost in a snagging survey or a homebuyer survey (see page 153): builders do make mistakes
Post-war homes	• Use relatively modern construction techniques • Tend to be a good size with reasonable gardens • Usually built of good quality brick	• Tend to be on sprawling estates • Some of the 1970s homes were built with 'new' materials, which haven't always stood the test of time	• Can be very good value for money, especially if they are ex-council houses that have now been 'sold' off
1900–1940	• Usually well built and of reasonable size • 1930s homes were some of the first to be built with some building regulations • Usually good solid walls with sound insulation • Good-sized gardens and driveways for those built after the 1930s • Often near to transport links	• Period features, such as stained-glass windows, can be expensive to maintain/replace • Can require a fair amount of maintenance	• Tend to be good value for money, even within expensive locations • Often semi-detached • Can feel a little 'estate like'
Pre 1900s	• Can be very attractive and characterful • Original features sometimes still present	• Layout may not suit lifestyle, e.g. kitchens can be small or there are '2+1' bedrooms – you have to go through one to get to another • May require regular maintenance	• Some may be **listed**, meaning you need to apply for permission for maintenance and any changes (see page 149) • Tend to be more expensive as there is a finite supply

NEW TRENDS

Private builders are often obliged to include a wider range of properties, including starter homes in 'mixed developments', in return for receiving planning permission. The government has announced a major building programme and other support for home buyers, particularly key workers such as nurses and teachers, backed by the statement: 'A fundamental principle of sustainable communities is that everyone should have the opportunity of a decent home at a price they can afford, in a place in which they want to live and work.' (For more information, see page 139.)

New properties

Buying a new property could allow you to meet many of the requirements on your needs and wants lists. First, developers tend to gear their properties to what the market is demanding, and also, if you get involved early enough, you can influence the planning and layout of your new home. There are a number of benefits to buying new properties (see the box, page 128).

If you opt for a new-build property, do not use a legal firm provided by the developer as there is potential for conflict of interest. Get an

Jargon buster

Buying off plan When you buy a property that hasn't been built yet, i.e. you are buying it based only on what you can see on the plans

Listed properties Buildings of historic interest are protected by the 'listing' process, which means owners must seek permission for any changes to the inside or outside of their building. For more information, see page 149.

New build A home that you buy from new or build yourself

Snagging These are checks for defects after a home has been built, extended or renovated

❝ If you are buying a new home, you may be able to become involved with decisions on planning and layout. ❞

independent specialist who is experienced in this area, and familiar with issues such as whether the property is correctly built on its allocated plot.

 For more information on older properties go to www.periodproperty.co.uk and www.lpoc.co.uk – the Listed Property Owners Club – where you will find plenty of specialised advice.

Advantages of buying new properties

Guaranteed purchase

- Once you have agreed the deal, you can exchange quite early on and secure the purchase
- If you value peace of mind, this is a big plus, but do check the builder can't pull out – prices may have increased since they exchanged and they can then charge more

Ease of purchase

- The property you are buying will be the end of the chain, so there is less chance of a legal hold-up
- Some developers will part-exchange your property so you don't have the hassle of selling it (this is a particular attraction in a slow market or if you think your property may be hard to sell)
- Many also offer deals to help you with moving costs

An easier mortgage

- Some builders fix up mortgage facilities for a development, making it easier to arrange a loan of a high percentage of the price. It won't always be the best deal available.

Extra features

- Fitted kitchens, bathrooms and flooring are often included in the price

Value for money

- Compared to period properties, new builds can offer a lot for the money

Design input

- If you buy **'off plan'**, when the property is at the design stage, you can have a say in the design, layout, fixture and fittings, so it will meet more of your needs and wants

Decoration

- The property will be freshly decorated, and you may be able to choose colours and styles of decoration if you buy early enough in the build

Lower upkeep

- New buildings will conform to high standards of insulation, making them energy efficient and less expensive to run
- Maintenance costs should also be low for the first few years because everything was installed new

Disadvantages of buying new properties

Faults

- This is a major issue as an average of 80 defects were found in new homes in 2005 even though most had already passed an inspection
- Nine out of every ten new homes has faults requiring attention
- Some of these are minor, but they mount up and add to the hassle of moving in: you want a new home, not be part of a building site (see the box on snagging, overleaf)

Price

- You do pay for the extras in the initial price and may have to wait a few years for the price of a new property to move into line with the local market
- If you have to move sooner, you might not get as much as you paid for it

Timing

- You may have to wait while the property is finished, and this can be delayed

Room size

- Some show homes are fitted with smaller-than-average size furniture to make the rooms seem larger
- Make sure your furniture will fit where you want it

Garage size

- Single garages can struggle to accommodate some vehicles; check yours will fit

What will it be like?

- When buying 'off plan' from a brochure it can be hard to picture room proportions, the size of the garden and how close neighbouring properties will be

Fittings

- There won't be many fittings, such as cupboards and shelves, which are often part of the deal on an existing property

Living on a building site

- Your home may be finished, but if the rest of the development isn't, you will be living with noise and dirt until the contractors are off site

Nag about snags

Snagging is the term used for finding the defects after a home has been built. You must have your own independent survey carried out on a new property to identify its faults, and there will be some. Examples include hot and cold taps being swapped, alarms that don't work, uneven floors, poor carpentry, scratched glass or worktops and incomplete damp courses. When you negotiate the contract, ask if you can set an amount or percentage of the price to be held back until all defects are dealt with.

When the faults have been fixed, check again for cosmetic damage and any fresh leaks or problems before approving the work. Your developer is liable for defects discovered during the first two years of your warranty, so report any in writing as soon as you are aware of them. This doesn't cover fair wear and tear.

For more information, see www. inspectorhome. co.uk.

Guarantees and insurance

New homes are not protected by the 1979 Sale of Goods Act or subsequent laws. Instead, protection on new homes is provided by a ten-year warranty from the National House Building Council (NHBC), Zurich Municipal or Premier Guarantee (for details, see box opposite).

The warranties offer protection if the builder goes bankrupt while building the property, for defects that become apparent within two years of completion, and for structural flaws for a further eight years. While these are better than nothing, the fairly weak level of guarantees and the hassle of having work done after you move in underline the importance of having an independent survey done even on newly built properties.

BUYING A PLOT OF LAND AND BUILDING YOUR OWN HOME

With the popularity of property TV programmes such as *Grand Designs* and *Property Ladder*, many people are gaining confidence in designing their own property either from scratch, or mostly from scratch. If you are considering finding a property to renovate, convert or buying a plot of land, then be prepared to:

- **Put the time aside you need** – it may literally take years.
- **Move away from where you are now,** unless there is plenty of land around you.
- **Find specialist companies** to work with as the finance, legal element, survey, planning and building regulations, and the price you pay will each require specific knowledge and someone that is used to dealing with 'non-standard' buying and selling.

Searching for land

The first steps are finding the best places to buy land. Try talking to local estate agents and surveyors as they should know the local market and if there are plots available. *Grand Designs* magazine may have information on local possibilities. There are also website services, such as www.plotsearch.co.uk, www.selfbuild.co.uk and www.plotfinder.net. However, unlike the free searches from companies such as Rightmove or Fish4homes (see page 136) you are likely to have to pay a subscription fee. This can vary tremendously from £20 through to £100 or more a year.

The other problem with these databases is that you don't know how good they are until you subscribe and there are also surprisingly few opportunities available for purchasing land. However, some of the good ones are worth the money, even if you only use them for research purposes. They can help you understand which areas you should start looking in, what sort of prices you are likely to have to pay, and how different areas compare in price. As there is such a shortage of land, some self-builders look to buy a plot with a property they can pull down. As renovating property is increasingly popular, too, many of the

finding facilities are adding these to their portfolio.

The main things to look out for when choosing databases to work with for finding land are:

- **How up-to-date** the information is (and how it is kept current).
- **Whether the land** included is agricultural (and therefore unlikely to receive planning permission) or already has outlined or even detailed planning permission.
- **Whether the subscription** is lifetime or annual. Lifetime is best due to the time it could take you to find that plot of land.
- **Ability to contact** the company for any help.

> **“** Find specialist companies to work with as the finance, legal element, planning and building require specific knowledge. **”**

Buying the land

The second issue you will have is that not all lenders will lend for land, building, converting or renovating property, so you will need to find specialist lenders to help you.

Websites for companies you can contact concerning protection on new homes are: www.inspectorhome.co.uk; www.nhbc.co.uk; www.premierguarantee.co.uk and www.zurich.co.uk.

It is worth talking to an independent financial adviser to help you get the best deal or go to a specialist company used to dealing with self-build, conversion and renovation projects.

Fortunately, the days of having to live in a caravan or tent on site are a thing of the past as the market has grown and companies have developed better offerings to help support you. So when you are looking for finance, make sure that:

- **You have the option** of staying in your home.
- **They understand** that costs may rise during your project.
- **They can help** you at every stage of the move.
- **Depending on your** financial circumstances, they lend the money up-front rather than bit by bit or only after you have purchased your land.

Getting a survey

Make sure that you get a good survey on the land: just because it looks okay to build on, doesn't mean it is. You don't know what's underneath! So do your research and get specialist surveyors and conveyancers to advise before you buy. Don't forget, too, that you may have to gain planning permission or a view from the local planning department before you purchase too. The planning offices are usually very helpful and local records will tell you if anyone has applied and been rejected or accepted before, so don't be afraid to pick up the phone and chat to them. They may even visit the land/property for you.

Use professionals

Finally, when you come to your build, make sure you shop around for services from an architect, project manager or builder. It is good to try to get an independent estimate on what your build might cost. Sometimes you have to pay a few hundred pounds for this, but there are companies that offer this service for free. When it comes to buying your materials, don't be afraid to go to the large merchants – such as Jewson, Wolseley and Travis Perkins – as you may well gain better prices than you would via your builder or project manager. The key message is: shop around or check out the quotes with an independent professional before you agree to them.

 Self-build websites to consult include: www.buildstore.co.uk; www.fmb.org.uk, www.labc-services.co.uk and www.planningportal.gov.uk. There are also a growing number of shows and centres that you can visit to help find out much more about how you build or renovate property. Most of these are held at Excel in London or the NEC in Birmingham, so check out www.buildstore.co.uk, www.excel-london.co.uk and www.necgroup.co.uk/whatson.

Choosing your location

Choosing the right location is sometimes more important than selecting the right style of property, because where you live has a big impact on the lifestyle of everyone in the home.

If the people in your household go out a lot locally, to the shops, pubs, leisure centres or other amenities, they'll want to be able to walk or have an easy drive. An edge of town setting is probably better for you than a home in the middle of the countryside, however idyllic it seems. Similarly, a regular commuter needs to consider the ease of their journey. Is it easy to reach the station? Will your car be crawling across a congested town centre twice a day to get to the main route out? What are the bus routes like?

Traffic is a major issue that can often be overlooked because we tend to view properties at the weekend. Visit the location at different times of the day and on weekdays as well as Sundays. Rush hour can turn the quietest road into a noisy race track. Speed-reducing humps in the road are a telltale sign that it is a rat run for passing traffic. However, there can be other causes: a popular venue for car

boot sales could mean there's a queue of vehicles outside your front door on Sunday mornings. Shift patterns in local factories, or being near a school, can cause sudden gluts of traffic – fine if you're always out, but a nuisance if that's when you often start or finish your journeys.

Heavy local traffic is noisy, but there are plenty of other sources of noise: a seemingly peaceful pub might have

The highlighter method

When buying a property, buy a street finder map (estate agents often give out local maps) for your target area. Driving or walking around the area will help you identify specific streets or zones that meet your requirements, including the type of property, or that you just like the 'feel' of. Highlight them on your map so you can quickly spot if new properties on the market are well positioned.

 You can research traffic issues by visiting the area at different times of day. Other drawbacks call for different research – see page 147 for matters such as subsidence and flooding.

Ask the light questions

The presence of natural light adds to our quality of life and it is important to consider where the property is in relation to the sun. Any room that never gets any sun is likely to feel dark and gloomy, especially in the winter. East-facing rooms get the morning sun (ideal for kitchens), while facing south or west brings some sun for most of the day. So similar houses on opposite sides of a road will feel very different.

loud music and an extended licence, which means your road resonates like a disco at midnight. It's no fun trying to work or rest at home against a pounding background of heavy machinery from a factory or garage.

NEW AREA?

If you are moving to an area you don't know, the best source of information is local people. So visit the area, pop into shops, pubs and information offices, if they have them, and ask, for example, what it's like to live there, which are the best areas, what the crime rate is like. You can ask to be sent copies of the local newspaper (they may make a small charge), and internet searches may well find local community websites, which will give you many insights. Good estate agents should be able to give you a fair briefing, too. Try websites such as www.upmystreet.com and www.neighbourhoodstatistics.co.uk.

BORDER COUNTRY

You can get a very good deal if you live close to the border of an area with very good amenities and schools. The property will cost less, the council tax is likely to be lower but you will benefit from good services. If choice of school is an important factor in your location, check the catchment area and the policy and availability of places – you can live in a catchment area but still be denied a place if the school or a certain year group is full (see also page 80).

Local factors have a big impact on property prices

Prices will be higher near:	Prices will be lowered by proximity to:
• Highly regarded state schools	• Noisy pubs and other entertainment venues
• Good leisure facilities	• Takeaways with rubbish left close by
• Convenient shopping	• Busy roads and flight paths
• Quality food stores	• Railway lines
• Good local transport	• Waste dumps and derelict land
• Pleasant countryside and parks	• Poorly regarded schools
• Well-maintained private housing	• Prisons
	• Masts and pylons
	• Local authority housing

Finding a property

The most traditional way of finding a property is to go through an estate agent. However, this is not the only means - local newspapers and auctions are the most obvious alternatives, but there are others, too, which are each described in this section.

THROUGH AN ESTATE AGENT

You can sell your house without an estate agent, but it is unlikely that you will buy without one as more than nine out of ten properties are sold through agencies. The key to getting the best out of an agent is to be prepared and to be straightforward. Before seriously briefing an agent on what you want, get your finances in place, including your Mortgage Agreement in Principle (MAP) (see page 40), and prepare your brief of what you really need. Look for agents who sell the types of property you want – check websites and local newspaper advertisements (see also pages 84–5).

A good agent will ask for information that will tell them how serious you are about buying. This will influence the level of service you get, because you don't pay them and they'll only want to put in effort that might result in a sale. Be honest: estate agents don't have the best reputation for truthfulness, but most can provide a long list of lies they've been told at this stage. They'll want to know:

- Is your property on the market? How close are you to a sale?
- Have you got a MAP or are you a cash buyer?
- What are you looking for?
- How much can you afford?

❝ The key to getting the best out of an estate agent is to be organised, prepared and to be straightforward. ❞

As discussed already, your brief should not describe your ideal home, but be a wide list of the types of property, locations and features that you are looking for, together with the reasons. For example, explain that you need a big garden for your dog, or a double bedroom because your children like to share their room. Print a copy for them to keep. The most common mistake people make is to rush into briefing an agent on their perfect home, then start backtracking later when they realise their needs are different, or they can't fund it.

The agent will supply you with details of properties within about 10 per cent of your price range. You can probably download details from their internet site, but also call each week to check if anything has just come on the market and not been through the system yet.

> ❝ Putting the word about that you are interested in buying could lead to a sale without the property even reaching the market. ❞

If you make an appointment for a viewing and can't make it, tell the agent. They'll appreciate you not wasting their time and being able to keep the seller informed. If a property suitable for you suddenly comes on the market and they need a quick sale, they're more likely to contact you if you are well organised and flexible than if they come to see you as a time-waster.

OTHER WAYS OF FINDING A PROPERTY

There are alternatives to estate agents, and most people start their search on the internet where there are agents' and private sale sites (see box, top right). This is a good way to start

getting a 'feel' for the market. In addition, there are several other routes that might lead to a private sale.

Local newspapers

Sellers marketing their own property are likely to advertise in the local property newspapers or publications such as *Loot*. Papers will send copies to your address if you don't live locally – there may be a small fee for this.

Your own contacts

Everyone has their own network of friends, contacts and relatives. Putting the word about that you are interested in buying could lead to a private sale without the property even reaching the market.

 To find local papers in an area, check the website www.newspapersoc.org.uk (the Newspaper Society), which allows you to search for daily and weekly local papers, both paid for and free.

Employers

Many firms have noticeboards and you may be able to advertise your interest in local property. Large companies have human resources departments who will be aware of anyone leaving, or perhaps relocating within the firm to another site. It costs little to ask for this information and you could strike it lucky. It's possible the company has agreed to sell their employee's home as part of a relocation package, in which case they'll be delighted to hear from you.

Notes through doors

This can be very productive. Everyone likes being complimented on their home, and a polite note put through the door saying how much you love it and if they would tell you if and when they'd like to sell might prompt someone into offering you a property. This is particularly worth trying when there is a shortage of your preferred property type.

Auctions

Auctions are undoubtedly a source of some cheap property, but you have to know what you are doing, because you have to spend money up front on a survey and legal checks before even bidding. Some 30,000 properties are sold by auction each year (just under 2 per cent of the market) – some homes may have been repossessed, some where the owner died without a will, and standard homes or properties that are likely to attract very little or a great deal of interest. You must get a survey on any property you buy through auction – before you bid.

> **"** Auctions are undoubtedly a source of some cheap property, but you have to know what you are doing because you have to spend money up front. **"**

You have to hand over 10 per cent of your successful bid on the day and pay the balance within 28 days. You can offer bids in advance and if the property is listed as 'unless previously sold', the seller may take your offer to save the trouble and expense of the auction process. Don't go down the auction route unless you definitely have the cash – including the full backing of any lender. Set a bidding limit of what you can afford and don't exceed it – if you're worried about getting carried away in the excitement, get someone you trust to do the bidding for you.

Websites giving auction details include www.eigroup.co.uk, www.ukauctionguides. co.uk and www.wheresmyproperty.com. Property Auction News magazine covers this field, too: www.propertyauctionnews.co.uk.

DISCOUNTED PROPERTY

Getting property at a discount is a full-time job for an expert unless you are very lucky. The first step is to know the local market inside out, so that you know the genuine value of the property types and locations in which you are interested. Experts suggest that about one in every 50 properties they view turns out to be a bargain – and they will already have vetted many from the particulars.

All the non-agent methods listed above should offer some kind of discount because the seller is not paying commission to an agent. Indeed, auction properties are more than a third cheaper than similar ones bought through high street agencies.

> **"Talk to property developers who are offering part-exchange deals to encourage buyers for their estate."**

But not everyone is willing or able to wait for the right property to come up at auction and risk money on what could be a wasted survey. By keeping in contact with estate agents you stand a good chance of hearing about a price being reduced due to a seller needing to move quickly because of a change in circumstances. Other reasons for discounted sales are:

- **Repossessions,** when the loan company takes over a property and will want to get rid of it quickly.
- **Relocations,** when someone needs to move to a new job. Large firms that offer relocation packages to senior staff are prepared to sell fast.
- **A chain collapsing** and a seller needing a new buyer quickly to ensure their own purchase goes through. This can be caused by a buyer dying, separating from a partner or hitting financial problems. In such circumstances you become the hero who saves the day.

Another route is to talk to property developers who are offering part-exchange deals to encourage buyers for their estate. They will be keen to sell the homes their buyers have left as quickly as possible, and that may mean the price is right for you.

Front of the grid

You can put yourself in a position to take advantage of any good deals that become available by selling your property and renting until the right home comes up at a good price. You can then put yourself on the front of the starting grid by making an offer as a cash buyer. However, there are increased costs involved, so make sure it's worth your while.

Unable to afford a property?

If you can't afford a property, maybe you are being too ambitious in your choice of home: if you own one already, perhaps you could extend it if space is the reason for moving. If you don't own anywhere, there are various schemes to encourage first-time buyers into the market, depending on the criteria you fit into.

SCHEMES TO HELP LOWER INCOME GROUPS

The Housing Corporation is a government-run body that funds and regulates housing associations in England, and there are similar bodies for other parts of the UK (see page 140). It has a number of schemes designed to help people on low incomes to buy property (see the Jargon buster box, right).

If you want to buy but can't afford it, you may be better off waiting. First, your pay may rise or you may decide to live with a partner, sharing the costs of buying. Second, if you are likely to move within a couple of years, perhaps for a new job, it might not be worth even considering buying because of the added costs (such as the survey, stamp duty, removals) that you never get back, compared to the more predictable costs of renting.

At the end of 2005, the government launched the Homebuy scheme, to help social tenants and key workers buy housing association property, newly built stock, or property

on the open market, which aims to help 100,000 households buy their own home by 2010.

Council house tenants may also be able to purchase their home under the Right to Buy scheme. Similar to the Right to Acquire scheme (see above), it

139

isn't an automatic right, and you must have been a council, housing association or armed forces tenant for at least two years if your tenancy started before 18 January 2005, and five years if it started on or after this date.

> " Pooling your resources with one or more friend or relative could give your finances the kick-start they need. "

CAN YOUR FAMILY HELP?

There may be someone in your family who has funds available to lend you your deposit or to guarantee your mortgage.

BUYING WITH OTHER PEOPLE

Pooling your resources with one or more friends or relatives could give your finances the kick-start they need. Many lenders won't consider more than two people for a mortgage together, although it is possible for up to four people to jointly own a property. If you are to be joint owners, you'll need a legal agreement establishing how ownership is shared. This is crucial because at some stage one of you is likely to want to leave. It's a two-way choice:

- **Joint tenants** have equal rights to the whole property and if one dies, the other inherits it, irrespective of the will of the deceased.
- **Tenants in common:** each have a specific (not necessarily equal) share in the property, which, in the event of one dying, will go to whoever is named in their will.

If you have a joint mortgage, you will both be responsible for the monthly payments, even if one of you leaves – so one person can be saddled with the whole mortgage, or perhaps worse, has to sell the property. None of the joint owners can be forced to leave, and the property can only be sold with agreement of them all. They should make a legal agreement about how to split the proceeds if they do agree to sell as otherwise they could end up arguing over it in court.

Sharing the costs of buying property might give you a dream start in home ownership, but the reality of sharing it 24/7 might turn it into a nightmare. You must agree in writing and in advance what you would do if someone wants to move out or sell up. This agreement should set out how you would value the property, each person's share, and how much notice to leave or sell you will give.

 Housing advice and housing association websites include: www.direct.gov.uk; www.housingcorp.gov.uk; www.housinginwales.co.uk; www.icsh.ie; www.nifha.org; www.oasis.gov.ie; www.odpm.gov.uk; www.sfha.co.uk; www.shelter.england.co.uk.

BUYING TO RENT OUT A ROOM

There is a growing trend for people to buy a property and cover some of their costs by renting out an extra room. This might be a better option than joint ownership as although you still have to share your home with someone, you are the owner (although you are also the landlord). There are specialist lenders who will fund loans on this basis. This arrangement can be helpful because it enables you to afford a larger, higher value property (for example, a two-bedroom flat instead of a bedsit), but leaves you in control. If your lodger leaves, you just need to replace him or her rather than sell up or buy their share of the property.

❝ If you are struggling to fund a purchase, you might want to consider renting out a room to help meet the costs. ❞

OFF TO THE PARK

A growing trend in the UK property market is for elderly people to buy a park home. This is either a permanent construction, usually a bungalow, or a large static caravan, located in a private park setting. In 2002, more than 120,000 people were living in park homes in England and Wales alone, and the figure is rising. Park homes attract those who wish to downsize to a smaller property and to whom the private, rural setting appeals. Typical sizes are 11 x 4m (35 x 12ft), giving a larger living space than many flats. There are often age restrictions, and many parks do not accept resident children or pets.

 Some park home information sites include www.iphas.co.uk; www.odpm.gov.uk; www.theparkhome.net and www.ukparks.com. Some offer more specialised information than others, but it's worth taking a look at them all.

Viewing property

Just as you probably have an emotional link with your own home, so the heart can rule the head when viewing. It can also be tricky wandering around an unfamiliar property with a stranger, whether it is with an agent or (potentially more embarrassingly if you don't like the place) the owner.

Viewing is easier with someone else to share impressions with, and to interact with the guide if you find it difficult. If a property meets your needs but the particulars don't appeal, view it anyway – it might turn out to be your dream home.

You do need to consider the ambience of the place and whether it could ever feel like home, but there are practicalities to consider, too. Take a printout of your 'needs' list and tick off or add a comment against each one as you explore the property.

A checklist for viewing

Use this checklist to act as prompts for what to look at when viewing a property.

Outside	Look for
Front – garden, entrance Roof Brickwork Chimneys Drains and gutters Window frames	• Tidiness, cracked or broken surface • Missing tiles • Wear, cracks, bulges • Crookedness, damp bottom bricks • Leaks and cracks • Paintwork, signs of rot
Inside, by room	Look for
Decoration Power sockets TV point Storage Flooring Evidence of damp Central heating Room size/layout	• Quality and condition (can you live with it for a while?) • Number and location, age of electrical system • Location • Is there enough, or potential for it? • Quality and condition (does any need replacing?) • Condensation, mould, fresh paint (see box, opposite) • Age of boiler and age/condition of radiators • Possibilities for knocking through

It is especially important to consider the layout. For example, some Victorian properties have a third bedroom, which can only be reached through another room, which can be very inconvenient.

Try to ignore the décor; it is the easiest thing to change if you don't like it. If it is not to your taste, it could put you off an otherwise suitable property. Bear in mind the points in the checklist for viewing, opposite.

❝ If the property has been on the market for more than 12 weeks, it suggests there could be a problem with selling it. ❞

Don't be wet

Water damages buildings so when you are viewing a property, look for signs of damp such as its distinctive smell, plaster coming off the walls, and if any wallpaper or paint is peeling. Damp can be disguised by special paint, so be suspicious of any patches of fresh paint, especially if they are in corners and on ceilings.

SOME PRACTICALITIES
Be as 'hands on' as you can:

- **Run the hot tap** to see how long it takes for hot water to arrive. In new houses, check the hot and cold taps are correctly fitted.
- **Check that the light** switches work.
- **Where is the boiler** and when was it last serviced? Have the sellers got the paperwork to prove it?
- **Where is the fuse box** and when was it last checked?
- **Where is the water stopcock?** Is the water metered?
- **Do the windows** open and shut properly?

Also see overleaf for questions to ask the vendor or agent who takes you around the property. After you have finished viewing any property, keep the details, including your notes. This can help you make comparisons and could be useful if, for example, a property that has been sold after you viewed it unexpectedly returns onto the market.

Such a file is also useful when speaking with agents as you can give the addresses of properties you do or don't like – it will help them gauge what might interest you.

 It is only when you have decided on which property you would like to pursue that you need to start concerning yourself with the content of the HIP, if there is one, and other more detailed information such as flooding and subsidence - see pages 146-50.

What to ask the vendor or agent

Ask the right questions and you will learn a lot more about the property than by just looking around it.

"How long has it been on the market?"

Anything more than 12 weeks suggests there could be a problem with selling the property. For example, it may be overpriced.

"How many people have viewed it?"

Again, a high number of viewings with no offer suggests that the property isn't being viewed by the right people, or that there may be an issue with the property.

"Have any offers been made and/or accepted?"

This will tell you the degree of genuine interest. Rejected offers suggest the property might be overpriced or faulty. Please bear in mind it is against the law for an agent to tell you how much someone else offered on the property.

"Have any sales fallen through? Why?"

There are many reasons a sale could have collapsed. If it was clearly the buyer changing their mind or not having the finance ready (both very common), that need not reflect on the property. If they pulled out for unspecified reasons, be alert for why this might have been.

"Has the vendor got a property to move to?"

This will help inform you how serious the vendor is – people do change their minds – although the HIP ought to show their commitment to selling. A vendor keen to move to a property they have offered on might be prepared to drop the price.

"Why is the vendor moving?"

Most people move as they are expanding or decreasing the family size, or moving in together for the first time. However, sometimes people move due to problems with neighbours or noise. Buying from vendors who are separating can slow the process as they might not be communicating or in agreement.

"What is included in the price?"

This is important as there may be fixtures and fittings you don't want (and therefore don't want to pay for) or do want but they are not part of the deal.

"Would the vendor negotiate on the price?"

A good agent will have discussed a minimum price the vendor might accept, so it is worth asking the agent who is selling the property as you may be given a steer.

"Can I see the Home Information Pack?"

See pages 105–8.

WHEN DO YOU KNOW IT'S THE RIGHT ONE?

Some people comment that they 'just fell in love with' the house they bought. There is certainly a place for gut feeling, but this is a big, expensive decision and it pays to be rational, too. Don't commit yourself to the first property you view: compare it with at least another five as it will help you decide if the one you like represents value for money. Arrange a second viewing, preferably at a different time and on a different day (so you can see how the light is different and what traffic and noise levels are like then). Take along your most sceptical friend who can be relied on to make challenging observations

Go over the advice on location on page 133 and try to check traffic and noise conditions at different times of day. If you don't do this then you could get a nasty shock when you move in and discover that traffic jams form outside your home twice a day, meaning you can't get out or park on your return, or noisy neighbours regularly have parties at night.

Find more detail on the property (see below) and when you are really confident you've found somewhere that meets your 'needs' requirements (and maybe a few 'wants'), is in a

The square foot test

The square foot test helps you decide if a house is good value for money. Calculate the square footage of the property from the layout or from the room dimensions, and divide it into the asking price (see page 88). This will give you a cost per square foot. Do the same with other properties you viewed or have details of so that you can make a comparison. This is useful as it is completely objective and helps to show how much space you are getting for your money.

“ Try to check traffic and noise conditions at different times of day – otherwise you could get a nasty shock when you move in and discover traffic jams forming outside your home twice a day. ”

suitable location and offers good value for money, you're should make some more specific checks.

 Find more detail on a property you are interested in, including the price it sold for last time, by looking at websites such as www.rightmove.co.uk and www.ourproperty.co.uk or for £2 at www.landreg.gov.uk.

Buying a property

Checking out a property

However much you like a property and are tempted to make an offer, it makes sense to make a few basic checks first. This saves time in the long-term because it will alert you to any problems that may put you off the purchase altogether, and it will help you to make an offer that reflects the value of the property.

Before June 2007 and the introduction of Home Information Packs (HIPs), your initial checks should include a basic search for environmental risks (see opposite page) and a double check on the location (see page 133). Find out the prices of other local properties by typing the postcode into one of the property valuation sites (see box below). This will add to your knowledge of the local market.

After June 2007, you will also need to read the HIP, which should be available electronically or in printed form from the estate agent or vendor. See the description of the HIP contents on pages 105–8. The home condition report will give you a rough idea of the overall condition of the property, and remember it is not a valuation. The Office of the Deputy Prime Minister claims that it should be 'a mid-level survey like the current

homebuyer survey (see page 153) and will be no less detailed than that survey', and they suggest that you therefore don't necessarily need another survey unless you require a structural one. The legal elements should highlight any complications

Check the age of the HIP

You should get your legal company to check the Home Information Pack contents, particularly if the pack is more than three months old. During this time, things such as other people applying – and receiving – planning permission can change and this might affect your decision to purchase. The rule is that when the property goes on the market, the pack cannot be more than three months old, but when marketed it will last the length of the sale.

 These websites will give you some idea of the value of similar properties in your area: www.hometrack.co.uk, www.ourproperty.co.uk and www.rightmove.co.uk. See also the box on page 136.

with boundaries or environmental problems, but you will still need to research this further (see below).

It may be difficult to compare two properties using their HIPs because the document does not have a standard format and the exact contents may vary. However, as background information, this is a valuable document.

ENVIRONMENTALS

The three biggest risks to property are flooding, subsidence and radon.

Flooding

It can take a year to renovate a property after a serious flood, never mind the emotional and physical trauma you will suffer. Sea encroachment and coastal erosion threaten 1.5 per cent of the country while 7 per cent of the country is likely to flood at least once every 100 years when rivers burst their banks, and many more properties could suffer from flash floods. Around 5 million people, in 2 million properties, live in flood risk areas in England and Wales.

In addition to the risk of water invasion, such properties are more expensive to insure. Visit www.environment-agency.gov.uk for information on flood risk by postcode area. You can also contact

www.homecheck.co.uk for a free summary risk report or gain a more comprehensive assessment, including other risks, such as contamination, radon and subsidence (for £29, although your legal firm might do this as part of their search).

Subsidence

This is when a property has moved because the ground beneath it can no longer support it. It can be caused by building over old mineshafts, tree roots growing into foundations, or long-term drought drying out the soil. It is a rare, but serious problem and should be picked up in your survey. Subsidence creates sudden, large cracks in the walls.

Radon

Radon is a natural radioactive gas that is thought to represent a cancer risk

Policy decision

If the property you are purchasing is at risk from environmental factors and you are concerned about getting insurance, ask the owner what policies they have and who they are with. You may be able to continue cover in the same way with the same firm.

 You can get information from the Health Protection Agency radon hotline on 01235 822622 (www.hpa.org.uk/radiation/radon/index.htm) and www.environment-agency.gov.uk and www.homecheck.co.uk.

when inhaled in large quantities. Good ventilation in houses can stop radon gas building up and there is a simple test kit to assess build-up. New homes in high-risk areas (which are mainly but not exclusively in the southwest of England and west Wales) must meet building regulations designed to protect against radon build-up. For further information, see foot of page 147.

> **❝ The three biggest risks to a property are flooding, subsidence and radon – get them checked. ❞**

CHECKS AND GUARANTEES

Legislation introduced in January 2005 states that any but the most basic electrical work must be carried out by a competent person, who must provide a certificate of safety. To understand what you can and can't do in a property, visit the New Rules for Electricity in the Home at www.odpm.gov.uk, where you can download the details, or call 0870 600 5522 for a leaflet.

The seller's HIP should include safety certificates for recent electrical or gas work. For your own peace of mind, always get the gas and electrics checked once your offer has been accepted. Go to a specialist service that will check both. The electrical check should cost from £100, with the gas check from £55, depending on the area you live in. Visit www.gas-elec.co.uk for more information.

Ask which guarantees are valid on the property relating to any of the following: timber treatment, damp, the boiler, flooring and carpets.

Check if the company that provided the service is still trading, otherwise the guarantee may have no value. A good timber or damp treatment firm will give you a free estimate and details of work that needs to be done.

Preserve your HIP

If you buy the property, keep all paperwork relating to these checks and guarantees in your HIP file. Keeping this information will be valuable if you choose to sell the property in the future. If you don't keep it, and can't prove work or services are guaranteed, you could have to spend a lot of money having it done again.

For more information on gas and electricity checks, see www.gas-elec.co.uk; www.odpm.gov.uk has information and a leaflet on the rules for carrying out electrical work; www.niceic.org.uk is the website for the National Inspection Council for Electrical Installation Contracting; www.eca.co.uk is the electrical contractors association.

LISTED PROPERTIES

Listed buildings are deemed to be of architectural or historical interest and are protected by law from significant change. There are three levels of listing, from Grade I (exceptional interest), to Grade II (more than special interest – most listed residential properties fall into this category) to Grade III (of special interest, worth preserving). There are about 370,000 such properties in England and Wales, they are usually over 150 years old and form a valued part of the landscape. Owners of listed buildings cannot make changes that would alter the character of the property (inside or out) without obtaining permission from the local planning authority. These are unlikely to sanction altering the windows, installing new fireplaces or replacing internal walls, and may decide against other changes, such as fitting burglar alarms, TV dishes or aerials.

Listed buildings are likely to be highly attractive and tend to be sold at premium prices. They can be expensive to run as working on them requires specialist craftsmen. There is no difference in how they are bought or sold, but it is important to check the grade of listing and whether it applies to all or part of the property.

You should choose surveyors and legal firms with experience of such buildings.

Some localities known as conservation areas also have regulations banning anything changing their character, which can extend to refusal to allow trees to be cut down.

BUYING A FLAT

Flats and apartments are attractive purchases for anyone who wants to live near the buzz of a city centre or to whom 'loft-style living' appeals. Developers have converted old buildings into blocks of apartments, some of which have shared leisure facilities. Such properties appeal to those people who don't need lots of living space: those without children, and downsizers.

Buying a flat is more complicated than buying a house because someone else owns the rest of the building and the land it stands on. The owner is known as the **freeholder**, and the purchaser of the flat is the **leaseholder** for a specified period. Their responsibilities typically break down as shown in the box at the foot of the page overleaf.

When considering purchasing a flat, it is important to experience what noise levels are like between

Websites that have all sorts of different information about listed properties include: www.english-heritage.org.uk, www.heritage.co.uk and www.periodproperty.uk.

the properties (some are much better insulated than others) and to talk to fellow residents to discover how well people get on and how matters such as routine maintenance are handled.

The legal aspect of buying a flat tends to take an extra couple of weeks and be more expensive (from £100 extra) because there is more paperwork and there are more checks to do. Key questions to ask include:

- How are major one-off costs such as replacing the roof or windows covered?
- What are the service charges, what do they cover and are they likely to rise?
- How do I contact the freeholder or managing agent?

Always read the leasehold agreement and watch out for restrictions on things such as sub-letting a room, keeping pets, noise and where you can hang washing. Ask your conveyancer for a summary of key restrictions in case you missed something.

Also find out early on how long the lease has to run. You may have trouble getting a loan if it is less than 70 years, in which case you may want to investigate whether the freeholder would extend it. This is often a source of conflict between the two parties.

The Leasehold Advisory Service offers free independent advice on leases: see www.lease-advice.org.

Changes in leasehold law

Leasehold is essentially a 'right to live' somewhere for a fixed period, which was originally 999 or 99 years. However, due to various disputes between freeholders and leaseholders, especially regarding renewing leases, the Commonhold and Leasehold Reform Act 2002 gives leaseholders more say in extending the lease or purchasing the freehold. It also offers an alternative of '**commonhold**' as a way of collectively owning and managing a property without a time limit.

Freeholder and leaseholder responsibilities

	Responsible for
Freeholder	• Buildings insurance • Maintenance and repairs of the property's communal areas such as the roof and stairways
Leaseholder	• Ground rent • Service charges • Contents insurance • Costs of upkeep shared with other leaseholders

Making your offer

Some people find the negotiation stage exciting, others hate it. Try to distance yourself from your emotions and treat it as a business transaction – how would you behave if it was part of your normal job?

Many factors will influence how much you decide to offer for the property, including:

- **Local market conditions:** are they stable, rising or falling?
- **How long** it's been on the market.
- **Prices of similar properties**.
- **How many of your needs** the property meets.
- **How much** you like it.
- **The price per square foot.**
- **The 'fit'** you have with the vendor in terms of when you'd want to move.
- **If you are a cash or first-time buyer,** you are in a stronger position than someone with a property to sell.

Your offer will be subject to the survey and contract, so you are not legally committing yourself to this price. Given this, and knowing what you can afford, you might offer the asking price or a figure below it. When you make this offer to the agent explain your rationale: what is your evidence that it is worth less than the asking price? What flaws or concerns have influenced you? You might want to make your offer subject to certain conditions apart from the survey. For example, there may be a flaw you need reassurance on. In particular, you can set a deadline on when you will exchange and complete. Make these conditions explicit and in writing.

The agent is legally obliged to pass on your offer to the vendor in writing. Ask for a copy to ensure it happens and is accurate. If you offer below the asking price, expect to negotiate. Don't be offended if the seller simply rejects the bid. Go over your sums again and if you are sure you are right with the value, tell the agent you'd like to look at other properties. A good agent will be able to judge whether to advise the seller to negotiate or not.

The common scenario if there is not a vast gap between the asking and offer prices is to eventually split the difference. So if the seller wanted £200,000 and you offered £188,000, you might both be prepared to settle at £194,000. The sums of money are enormous and you must be sure you are happy with the price, because now you're going to be spending your own, non-refundable money to check out the purchase.

Getting a survey

The condition of the property affects its price. If you buy one in poor condition, you may get it below market price, but it may have already been adjusted down to take into account the money needing to be spent on it. The key is to know what is required.

After June 2007, much of this information should be in the HIP (see pages 105-8). However, you should also get your own independent survey done. This is not the same as the **mortgage valuation** your lender will arrange – that is simply a check that the property exists and is worth more than what they are loaning. If that valuation is at odds with what you have offered, you might not be able to go ahead. The lender may also set certain conditions, such as completion of a damp course, before agreeing the loan.

SURVEYS

You should commission your own independent survey, even if the property is newly built. Very often surveys identify faults that allow you to renegotiate the price, so they pay for themselves. You have a choice of two types – a **homebuyer survey** and a **buildings survey** – and the HIP will help you decide.

From June 2007, the HIP will include a **home condition report**, which is reasonably thorough (i.e. more than just a valuation survey to check the property exists) and is expected to cover everything that is in a homebuyer survey.

Jargon buster

Buildings survey Also called a structural survey, this provides a detailed report on the property's construction

Homebuyer survey A standard report that evaluates any urgent repairs

Home condition report A survey that is a part of the HIP and should be the equivalent of a homebuyer survey

Mortgage valuation A report commissioned by your lender to check the property is valued correctly

❝ You should always get your own independent survey done. This is not the same as the mortgage valuation. Very often a survey identifies faults that allow you to renegotiate the price. ❞

A homebuyer survey

This is suitable for post 1930s properties of standard construction that do not seem to have any structural problems. It covers the general condition of the property, including:

- Roof, chimney, tiles and flashing.
- Walls, floors and ceilings.
- Guttering and drainage.
- Windows and doors.
- Structure and build quality.
- Location and surrounding area.

You should investigate any particular problems highlighted, such as damp or rotting timber. It will usually be easier and cheaper to get the relevant specialist firm to advise on this, rather than employ a surveyor. You will not be able to employ the surveyor who produced the home condition report because of the potential conflict of interest. However, if there are structural problems, you may need to commission a fuller investigation, known as a building survey.

A homebuyer survey takes several hours and the average cost is £500. If you can, accompany the surveyor at this time because in this way you are bound to learn something about the property.

If you have noticed anything about the property that you think may be a problem, such as signs of damp, cracks or bulges in plaster or brickwork, brief your surveyor on this.

A buildings survey

This is a more thorough assessment suitable for older properties or anything of non-standard construction.

- It goes into more detail where necessary, for example, on the condition of the timber and whether there is evidence of pests.
- It involves more work than the homebuyer survey, and so will cost more (from £500 upwards).

When you receive the survey, read it carefully. Sometimes things seem worse when written down. But pay particular attention to the degree of concern expressed about any faults. Surveys often recommend specialist inspections of particular problems. Always follow these up. Tradesmen will give you a more accurate estimate free of charge, and you can get timber and damp surveys for free from firms specialising in their treatment. A sensible vendor who is aware of the problem will have obtained estimates on the work required to fix the problem, and you may be able to negotiate on who will pay, or whether the sale price needs to drop, assuming you still want to go ahead.

Check, too, that any boundary fences or walls match the boundary marked on the land registry map. It might not, especially on new and renovated property. Measure it and check it against the map – you could be paying for land the other side of the fence.

Buying in different markets

BUYING IN A STRONG MARKET

There are additional pressures when buying in a strong market: you can feel as if this is your last chance to jump on or up the property ladder before it gets yanked out of reach. When properties are selling fast and prices are rising, you need to be well organised and prepared.

- Be sure you have your finances in place and have a clear, wide brief for the agent. ✓

- Process paperwork fast. ✓

- Check that your vendor has a property to move to, or ask if they are prepared to move out and rent or stay with friends to complete the sale quickly. ✓

- Be careful not to choose an unsuitable property under pressure of rising prices: it will be hard to sell next time around. ✓

BUYING IN A FALLING MARKET

When prices start falling, you may feel that you could be paying too much for a property that will be worth less in three months' time. This may be the case, but remember why you are buying it (presumably because you really want to live there) and that in the long-term, prices have historically risen.

- Bear in mind that if you wait for prices to fall further, your own sale price could drop too. ✓

- If you can, sell up and rent or stay with friends for a while so that you can keep looking and go in as a cash buyer. ✓

- Expect to negotiate the price down, explaining your understanding that prices generally are dropping. ✓

Managing the chain

Property chains are the stuff of nightmares: so many people's lives can be adversely affected by one person's actions. This chapter explains how to find out what is happening up and down the chain and what you can do to keep things moving so that you get into your new home on schedule.

Running the chain gang

The chain is the series of buyers and sellers linked together because each is selling and purchasing a property from one of the others, apart from the people at either end. Property chains can put people off buying property, creating such a series of delays, confusion, stress and worry that many people swear 'Never again!' ... but often later find that they must go through it all once more.

Part of the problem is the number of people involved, none of them with a bird's eye view of the whole process. A typical chain in England or Wales features seven properties, each with at least one seller, plus their estate agent, legal firm, surveyor, lender, and other service providers. There could easily be 50 people involved, each with a crucial role at some point, and if one of them forgets to sign a piece of paper, loses a document, misses a phone message, neglects to check a detail, accidentally deletes all their emails, or disappears on holiday, the whole chain could be delayed. The impact of this on the buyers' and sellers' lives can be enormous. Added to this is the problem that property deals seem to bring out the worst in people: they can get very greedy and selfish, at a massive cost to others.

❝ There could easily be 50 people involved, each with a crucial role at some point. ❞

A property chain could form like this particular example:

- **A:** First-time buyer, purchasing a bedsit from ...
- **B:** ... a single woman trading up to a two-bedroom house owned by ...
- **C:** ... a couple moving to a three-bedroom house with room for their two young children. They are buying from ...
- **D:** ... a professional couple with children who are buying a four/five-bedroom property to which they will add a granny flat for his mother. They are buying from ...

 Be tenacious in your attempts to keep everything moving forwards. You can't be organised enough nor afraid to pester everyone involved in the chain - see pages 159-60 for advice on how to keep on top of everything.

- **E:** ... a couple who are separating and selling their home to finance two smaller properties, one owned by ...
- **F:** ... an older couple downsizing to a smaller bungalow on the coast currently owned by ...
- **G:** ... an elderly woman who is moving into a nursing home. The other property the Es are buying is a three-bedroom semi detached owned by ...
- **H:** ... a couple retiring to a Spanish villa being built by a developer.

Spend a moment thinking about each person in the chain and you can conjure up many reasons why they might change their mind, try to delay progress, or just run out of money. The chain will only progress at the pace of the slowest link. The tricky bit is knowing who that is at any one stage and encouraging them to get a move on.

HOW TO AVOID GETTING IN A CHAIN

With the right preparation and research, there are times when you can avoid being in a chain, or at least a long one.

- **Buy from a developer** offering part exchange, so they buy your property and there is no one further up the chain.
- **Sell your property** and go into short-term rented accommodation, or if you are lucky, house-sit a

friend's home or stay with friends or relatives. Then, as a cash buyer, choose vendors whose chain is short, or who are themselves prepared to move out and rent. You'll need to put a lot of your belongings into storage.
- **Buy an already** empty property.
- **If you can,** choose a buyer who isn't in a chain themselves.
- **Only make offers** where the chain is short.
- **Negotiate a move-in date** with your vendor, after which they are prepared to move out, whatever their circumstances, or the deal will be off.

❝ The chain will only progress at the pace of the slowest link. ❞

HOW TO KEEP A CHAIN MOVING

Buyers and sellers who are part of a chain often feel that it is the job of the professionals to keep communicating and ensuring the right things are happening: they feel excluded from the process. However, there is no formal structure to a chain and so it often comes down to pot luck and one individual taking it upon him or herself to check, remind and nag others to turn their paperwork around. Some agents do a good job here, and wise agents – big and small – have dedicated sales progression departments.

Why do chains fail?

- **Poor communication:** someone doesn't get around to signing or filling in a document, and no one chases them up.
- **A buyer or a seller** changes their mind about the deal and pulls out.
- **A buyer** can't get a loan to match the offer they made.
- **A legal firm** with too many cases on its books only reviews each case once a week, sends out the relevant letters, then only chases them up a week later after the next review.
- **A survey** reveals problems, which prompt the buyer to pull out or the mortgage company to hold back part of the loan.
- **The survey** requires further specialist surveys, such as timber and damp, or a structural engineer.
- **Couples split up** and pull out of a sale or purchase.
- **A buyer or seller** falls ill or loses their job, pulling out of a deal as a result.

> **❝** Some vendors seem to have no compunction about taking their house off the market at a surprisingly late stage. **❞**

GAZUMPING

Gazumping is when your vendor accepts your offer but then agrees a higher price with another buyer. It is not as common as media stories suggest, but it can happen. Prevent it by making your offer subject to the property being taken off the market for an agreed period while you both sort out the paperwork to exchange. As a vendor, make sure you only do this for someone who can prove they have a Mortgage Agreement in Principle and are in a position to purchase the property – such as a cash buyer.

Some vendors seem to have no compunction about taking their house off the market at surprisingly late stages. There is little you can do about this, but since their agent will not be paid unless the sale goes through (although the HIPs should help change this situation), in an ideal world they wouldn't market a property they did not believe the vendor wants to sell. Sadly this doesn't happen and the agent often gets caught out. Estate agents are legally obliged to pass on all offers, so someone who viewed the property before you put in an offer can still make a bid.

 The opposite of gazumping is gazundering. For more information, see page 205. If you feel you have been unfairly treated by an estate agent, go to pages 178-9 where there is information on dealing with disputes.

How to manage the chain

Look through the checklist that appears opposite for why a chain can fail and make sure none of it applies to you. You should also help the rest of the chain by making sure that you follow as much of the following information as possible.

- **Employ a good,** experienced agent and legal specialist.
- **Get your finances in place** early, especially cash for your deposit at time of exchange.
- **File everything,** including copies of your correspondence and notes of telephone conversations. Keep copies of contact details of services at work, just in case.
- **Have copies of documents** that are likely to be requested, such as planning permission, plans of drainage systems, etc,
- **Turn around** your paperwork promptly.
- **Deliver documents** by hand, courier or special delivery.
- **Put clauses** in your buying and selling contracts stipulating the dates by which you should exchange, have the survey done, and complete.
- **If you are part of a couple,** share out the jobs (it is quite surprising just how often people put down the phone to one party, then pick it up only to receive a call from its other half).

 If your survey reveals a problem that was not apparent in the HIP survey or your mortgage valuation, don't panic. All types of faults can seem horrendous in writing, but they can be fixed. Get a builder or specialist's opinion and discuss it with your vendor: they will want to be flexible to keep the sale going, so you should be able to renegotiate the price to allow for the work required.

We become more stressed if we don't know or understand what is going on, so get involved. Talk to your representatives regularly – at least once a week – and ask if there is anything they or you should be doing next and by when. Ask where there are problems and who should be dealing with them. If someone needs to be hurried along, ask if you are allowed to give them a ring, or who will and when they will get back to you. Keep a list of everyone's contact details (landlines, mobiles, faxes, email and postal addresses) so that you can get in touch if you need to. Be tenacious and proactive and try to treat the process as you would a business deal.

All this is going to take time, and be emotionally draining. If possible, reduce your other workload and commitments so that you are available – for example, put off foreign trips and don't go on a last-minute holiday to escape the stress! Be flexible: if your buyer finds flaws with the property, turn off the alarm bells in your head and consider the problem. You might be able to deal with it yourself or you might decide it merits negotiation on price. Remember that your agent will probably have come across such problems before and should have some advice: they are working for you.

❝ Be tenacious and proactive and try to treat the process as you would a business deal. ❞

GETTING TO THE EXCHANGE STAGE

Exchange of contracts is when the copies of the signed contracts are swapped between the two legal firms and a deposit is made by the buyer to the vendor. It is the point at which an agreement to buy or sell becomes a legally binding obligation. Once everyone in the chain has exchanged, you're on the home straight because no one can back out of their deal. At this point a date should be set for completion and a legal firm can be sued if they fail to meet that date, so they have a strong incentive to meet the deadline.

However, most delays occur on the route to exchange. All of these stages must be complete:

- **Property deeds** drawn down from the lender of the property for sale.
- **Preliminary enquiries** and local searches.
- **Fixtures and fittings form** and property information forms filled in and signed.
- **Survey** and any resulting actions or negotiations.
- **Other negotiations** (e.g. on fixtures and fittings).
- **Answers** to all 'buyers questions'.
- **Written mortgage offer.**
- **Contracts** for sale and purchase drawn up.
- **Agreed deposit** available.
- **Completion** date agreed.
- **Buildings insurance** in place by the buyer.

❝ Try not to complete on a Friday, because removals firms tend to be booked up on that day. ❞

When buying, you become legally responsible for the property's building insurance once you exchange, so you will need to have this arranged and pass the policy number and a copy of the policy to your legal firm. It is worth asking the vendor who their policy is with as you may want to continue with that insurer. This is a particularly good idea if the property is in a flood risk area or has subsidence problems as the insurer will already have details on the building and associated risks.

Faster with a HIP?

The HIP should make it easier to avoid delays as it contains some of the information listed opposite. However, a legal firm acting on your behalf may well want to check on many details, some of which will take weeks (like local authority searches), so not all sales will progress faster because of the HIP.

SETTING A COMPLETION DATE

There are many other jobs to do between finalising the legal agreement and moving in, so it makes sense to agree a completion date at least two weeks after exchange. Unless someone is going into rented or borrowed accommodation, everyone in the chain moves house on completion day, or a day or two after. Try not to complete on a Friday, because removals firms tend to be booked up on that day, and, also, if there are delays with finances, you could be stranded for a whole weekend and end up paying for your goods to be stored over that time. You also need to decide how you will move and choose a removals firm (see pages 166–7).

You may want to arrange to visit your new property so you can take measurements to see if your curtains and loose carpets will fit, and to check if there is room for your kitchen appliances, such as the fridge. You should also notify your 'contents' insurance provider of when and where you will be moving and check with them what is/is not insured during the move, as you may need to get additional insurance from them, or via the removal company (see also page 167).

 See pages 64-6 for advice on choosing buildings insurance. You won't be able to exchange contracts on a property until this is organised so you obviously need to get organised up front.

GETTING TO COMPLETION

Completion is when the remaining money is paid by the buyer and the mortgage company and you get the keys to your new property over which you took ownership when you exchanged. That's why you can't complete without having exchanged contracts, although on very rare occasions completion and exchange can happen at the same time. Your role in completion is to wait nervously for the phone call telling you all is well.

The money is paid from:

- **Any balance** left after your mortgage is paid off with the funds from your purchaser.
- **Your new loan.**
- **Your own cash.**

The money is transferred electronically between the legal firms' bank accounts, each one triggering the next transfer. This all takes time and if you are near the top of the chain, the system may run out of time in transferring funds, so have a contingency plan for where you could stay overnight if you have handed over the keys but have nowhere to go. This is another reason to try to avoid completing on Fridays, as unfinished business will then be left to the following Monday.

When selling, never hand over the keys until your legal firm tells you they have completed. Waiting for that call can be nerve wracking. If it doesn't come, call your legal firm and find out why. There could be a hitch, such as someone suddenly falling ill, in which case you may all have to wait another day. If this is the case, you may need to negotiate who is covering the costs of this, such as hotel and storage charges.

Buy some time if you can

The few days after you move into your new property are an ideal time to change any superficial decoration you don't like, put up new cupboards, curtains and some familiar pictures, and clean out anything that isn't up to your standards. If you are able to arrange a couple of days between completion and moving in (maybe with your belongings going into storage), you can get a lot done in an empty property.

❝ Have a contingency plan for where you could stay overnight if you have handed over the keys but have nowhere to go. ❞

162

Preparing for move day

Preparation is the key to a smooth moving day that is as stress free as possible. This chapter explains how getting professional help can save your sanity and your back. As always, who you choose is crucial and there is guidance on this, as well as how to stay organised in the run-up to the big day.

Getting organised

Moving day can be the day when all the stress of selling and buying a property is multiplied tenfold. You can do a lot to lower the anxiety levels, but they won't disappear altogether: it will be physically tiring and emotionally draining.

The first step can be taken weeks ahead of your move: clear out everything you don't use or need. You'll otherwise be paying money to move stuff that you don't want and which is going to clutter up your new home. With a bit of luck, you could raise enough at a car boot sale to pay your removals costs. Think about where your furniture will be going in the new property, and check that it will fit. If it won't fit, sell it, give it away or take it to the dump now. Check what you've got stacked in the loft and other storage spaces, such as the garage or shed, and dispense with what you don't need.

❝ Think about where your furniture will be going in the new property, and check that it will fit. ❞

You'll have to decide early on if you are going to use a removals firm, and if you are going to get them to do the packing. The decision is needed now because if you pack yourself, it could take weeks.

DO YOU WANT A REMOVALS FIRM?

If you live in a ground floor one-bedroom flat with little clutter, you can hire a van, get a couple of friends to help, and move yourself on the day. If you've got more than four rooms to empty, there's probably too much to do. Consider how many possessions you have. What's hidden away in the loft or the garden shed? It can come as a big shock to discover how many goods you have accumulated. Now imagine having to pick up each one of them, carry it across an obstacle course (including stairs) and put it down without breaking your back – and all to a deadline.

 Take a look at the countdown checklist on page 170 for prompts for what you need to be thinking about several weeks before the move itself. You can't start planning for the day soon enough.

MOVING YOURSELF

If you decide you can move yourself, book the largest van you can (anything over 7.5 tonnes when loaded requires an HGV licence). Ask for one with a low kerb height or a let-down tailboard for ease of loading. Remember you'll probably have to make several journeys, including a final one to return the van, so this is only practical for moves over a fairly short distance. Loading and unloading it will be tiring and you might not relish the subsequent unpacking and setting up required over the next few days in your new property.

Leader of the pack

A major disadvantage of packing yourself is the time it takes, leaving you in a sweaty panic on moving day, or doing without key possessions for weeks ahead of the move.

So, well in advance of the move, buy or hire packing cases – they are stronger than cardboard boxes and it's easier to pack containers of the same size. Start by packing the things you won't need before the move. Depending on the time of year, this could be gardening equipment, summer clothes, etc.

Wear gloves when packing – it's amazing how much dirt collects on your hands otherwise. Put layers of crumpled paper or other protective material between each item to prevent scratching. Check the box is not too heavy and label it clearly with its contents and which floor and room it should go to. Draw an arrow to show which way up it should be stored.

Don't overfill boxes with heavy items: put heavy things on the bottom and lighter items on the top. Keep hazardous substances such as household cleaners and decorating supplies in separate boxes to other goods and mark 'hazardous'.

When carrying heavy items, take extreme care and try not to put any strain on your back – keep it straight as much as possible. Watch out for jolts from uneven surfaces and things left on the floor.

> **"** It is worth labelling all boxes with a brief description of their contents and the intended room. **"**

Nuts and bolts advice

When dismantling furniture, put all the screws, nuts and bolts in a labelled clear plastic bag and tape it to one of the pieces.

Packing box suppliers include: www.helpineedboxes.co.uk, www.removal-supply.co.uk and www.ekmpowershop.co.uk. Or you can go into any storage company, such as Access or Big Yellow, and buy them from there.

Choosing a removals firm

Amazingly, only about a quarter of people moving opt for a professional, registered removal firm. Doing it cheaper yourself or by hiring a 'man with a van' can be a false economy. While the pressure to save money is understandable at this time, the cost in creaking backs and strained relationships is immeasurable.

Using a professional firm means:

- **Your possessions** are packed properly and insured in transit.
- **Trained staff** can pack fast, probably only a day or two ahead of the move.
- **You don't have to lift** and carry heavy or bulky items, so you are free to deal with the many other jobs that need doing before and on the day of the move.

There are plenty of horror stories about sloppy removals men, but most firms do a professional job. Go for a member of the British Association of Removers or one that is regulated by the Removals Ombudsman (see box, below).

Always get more than one estimate of the cost, preferably from someone coming to the property rather than going online. This is because there may be problems with access, or very tight stairways, which will affect the job. If you are moving to a new area,

Access problems

Heavy or tall lorries can't always cope with steep gradients, tight bends or uneven roads. Check if there are access or parking problems at the other end – you may need to contact the police to get permission to unload, or to have a parking meter suspended.

 Removals firm websites include: www.bar.co.uk (British Association of Removers); www.removalsombudsman.org.uk (check the firm you choose is a member); www.ngrs.co.uk (National Guild of Removers and Storers) and www.fidi.com (International Federation of International Furniture Removers) – specialists in moving overseas.

it may be worth getting an estimate from a firm based where you are going: prices there may be more competitive. Make sure you mention all the items you want moved: the contents of a loft, garage or shed, for example.

Ask for the estimate to be broken down so that you can see what you are paying for: insurance, packing, hourly rate, mileage and any storage costs. This will help you compare costs accurately. Find out if overtime rates apply and at what time they start. Ask what would happen if the move is delayed and you couldn't get into the new property in the afternoon or, worse, the next day. Check that they have adequate insurance cover and also what the time limit is on claiming on insurance after the move. If you have some high value possessions, check if they need special packing and if they will also be covered by insurance (some policies set a limit per item).

You can still choose to do some of the packing yourself, which will save on costs, but steer clear of packing breakables and remember the removal firms insurance will not cover items you pack. Ask your removals firm to supply packing cases a few weeks in advance, and if they can't, go to the websites listed on page 165. If the distance of your move is short, you may be able to transport some items yourself, which will also save on overall costs.

BRIEFING A REMOVALS FIRM

Once you have chosen the firm, prepare and send them a briefing sheet to include:

- **Any items** needing special packing, such as pictures, antiques and valuable objects.
- **Difficult to move** items, such as a piano or fish tank.
- **Wardrobes** or other large furniture that may need to be dismantled.
- **Any carpets** and curtains that are going.
- **Items** you will be taking yourself.
- **A layout** of the new property with rooms identified, so that they/you can label boxes with their destination. Colour coding can work well here as it is quick to do and easy to understand.

❝It may be worth getting an estimate from a firm based where you are going: prices there may be more competitive.❞

I'm moving

There is a vast list of organisations that you need to inform. It therefore makes sense to send them a standard letter with a gap for you to add relevant reference and account details. See the table on page 170 for suggested timings.

As well as all the organisations and people listed opposite, tell the post office so that mail will be redirected. You'll need a form available from www.postoffice.co.uk, by phone or from a post office branch. It takes about ten days to come into effect. Prepare change of address cards for friends and family.

If you are changing your phone number, you can also arrange for your telephone company to inform callers of your new number for a few weeks following the switch-over date.

TRANSFERRING SERVICES

Ten days ahead of your projected move, make sure all utility services, such as water, gas and electricity, are informed that you will be moving. Ask them to arrange to read the meters on the move day. Ring to check this will happen. If they can't, ask a qualified electrician to do a reading so that you

Freeze yourself out

Run down the contents of your freezer, and only buy fresh food for a few weeks before the move to help you to use up frozen and stored foods.

have an independent record or take a date-stamped digital photograph of your meter reading. Moving house is a good time to review your arrangements with utilities. You can check out the latest deals at www.which.co.uk/switch, www.uswitch.co.uk and www.buy.co.uk. You can transfer your landline phone number to your new address for a charge.

Most companies will have a special telephone number to call to advise that you are moving or you can contact them in writing and, more frequently, by the internet. Make sure

 www.iammoving.com will issue change of address details for you. They do this free of charge but may pass on your information for direct marketing purposes unless you specify that they can't. On the plus side, you may save some time, expense and hassle.

Organisations and people to contact with change of address details

As soon as you have an approximate idea of when you will be moving, it is worth contacting the following organisations – either email or a letter is the most efficient so that everything is clearly set out in writing. This list is by no means exhaustive; there are bound to be additions relating to your particular circumstances.

Government organisations

- Department for Work and Pensions
- Inland Revenue
- VAT office

Finance

- Your bank and credit card firms
- Savings and investment firms, such as National Savings and Investment Premium Bonds
- Pension services
- Store loyalty cards

Insurance

- Contents and building (and see car)

Suppliers

- Water, gas, electricity
- Landline phone and broadband company
- Sky/cable/TV licence
- Magazine subscriptions

Car

- DVLA, for both your licence and the vehicle registration, but don't do this before you move as you may need your licence for identification and van hire
- Car insurance, MOT
- Breakdown service

Health

- Doctor, dentist, optician, plus any others

Work, education and leisure

- Your employer and professional associations
- Your colleagues
- Schools and colleges
- Clubs
- Football pools
- Local newsletters
- Other mailing lists (theatres, catalogues, charities)

Countdown checklists

Four weeks ahead

- Get removals estimates and book your chosen firm (even with a provisional date)
- Order packing cases
- Order new curtains/carpets for the property
- Plan where furniture will go and dispose of unwanted items
- Book the days needed off work

Two weeks ahead

- Inform utility companies
- Complete the mail redirection form
- Inform TV signal supplier and TV licence
- Start packing non-essentials – start outside or at the top of the house
- Run down the freezer

One week ahead

- Inform the people on the finance and medical lists
- Tell your council and ask for a statement on your council tax – you may get a refund
- Inform the car and household insurance firms
- Send out change of address cards to friends and family
- Organise who will look after pets or children during the move
- Transfer into pots any plants you've said you will be taking

Two days ahead

- Defrost the freezer
- Prepare your 'essentials' box (see page 172)
- Set aside things you will be transporting
- Disconnect dishwasher (if removals men are not doing it)
- Label items and keys for the new owner

After moving

- Pay stamp duty land tax (see page 175)

you have a receipt or record of them being notified by you as the utility companies can make mistakes and if they do, you are still liable for the bill unless you can prove you notified them and they have received it.

INFORMATION FOR THE NEW OWNER

It is very helpful if you prepare a briefing sheet for the new owner. This should include how to operate the boiler and alarm, the location of the meters, fuse box and stopcock, and any other useful information. You could either label all keys or leave them in the lock that they operate. Don't forget shed and garage keys, or those for the window locks.

And don't forget to ask – or have it as part of your purchase agreement – that the person you are buying from does the same.

ON THE DAY

If you can take it, have a big breakfast as mealtimes are likely to be disrupted today. Put down cloths to protect the floor as people traipse in and out. The removals men are likely to turn up early and they work very fast, so if you are dismantling furniture or disconnecting appliances, do it before they arrive. Check the foreman knows the brief (give him a copy if necessary). Get his mobile phone number in case of emergencies (remember, you'll be travelling separately).

Strip the beds. Get the electricity and gas meters read (if it has to be you, get

someone to witness your reading and sign the paper, or take a photograph of the meter – it might help if there is a dispute). Set aside the vacuum cleaner and cleaning equipment for your last-minute clear up.

If you have young children, take them to whoever is caring for them until you move. Do the same with any pets. If you know where you are in the chain, you will have some idea of when you are likely to hear you have completed, as it will work up from the bottom. So if you are a first-time buyer at the end of the chain, you should be able to move as early as 12 noon. And if you are selling to first time buyers, be prepared to be out by then! The poor people further along the line will have to wait.

❝ Prepare a briefing sheet for the new owner with key information for keys and alarms. ❞

meal (and you might prefer a takeaway). You may realise you need to clean items such as kitchen cupboards or shelves before stacking anything in them. Take readings of any gas and electricity meters as a record in case of any dispute with the supplier. As with leaving your sold property, if possible, photograph the figures, or write them down and get someone to witness your writing.

Your removals team will expect a tip, and you will most likely feel they've earned it. If there is a problem with their work, tell the foreman. You may be asked to sign to confirm the job is completed (check the van!) and if you haven't yet inspected your belongings, note that they are unexamined. This will help if there is a dispute later.

Be prepared to feel tired and maybe a bit let down: you probably haven't seen the property empty or noticed blemishes on walls that were hidden behind furniture. Try to stay positive and remember what it is that attracted you to the property in the first place.

As soon as the house is empty, zoom around it for a last-minute clean up. Do not leave the house until your legal firm advises you to, and drop off the keys with the agent.

❝ Don't expect to unpack anything but the bare essentials: bedding and a meal. ❞

YOUR NEW HOME

When you get in, label or colour code each room so the removals men know what will go where. Be clear about where you want any heavy furniture put. Don't expect to unpack anything but the bare essentials: bedding and a

Settling in

It's not over yet! This chapter deals with the 'must do' jobs after moving in, and offers guidance on what you need to do from now on to make the preparation of your Home Information Pack easier next time round. This is also your chance to review how the move went and deal with any complaints or disputes with the other people and firms involved.

File your paperwork

Phew! Once you've had time to get used to your new home, think back over the whole selling and buying process and consider what went well and what didn't. What could you have done to make it easier? Did the people working on your behalf do a good job? If they did, make a note that you'd use them again and recommend them to friends. If they didn't, you may want to make a complaint.

The first thing to do is to file all the paperwork to do with the process. This will help you in making judgements about how to do it better next time, and also, very importantly, help you retain the information for the next time you sell your property. Your file will hold essential information for your next HIP, even if you don't move for ten years. So make sure you include in it:

- The sale particulars of your home
- The HIP
- All correspondence and notes about your agent
- All correspondence and notes about your survey
- All correspondence and notes about your legal firm
- All correspondence and notes about your mortgage
- Your buildings and contents insurance
- Any estimates from builders and other tradesmen for work to be done
- Safety certificates, warranties and guarantees.

You should also keep an ongoing record of any decoration you undertake. This should include the source and code numbers of paints, flooring and carpets. You'll be grateful for this when you want to touch up the paintwork in three years time and can't remember which shade it was!

“ Your file will hold essential information for your next HIP. ”

 The stamp duty land tax help line is 0845 603 0135 or website www.hmrc.gov.uk. To contact the Land Registry go to www.landregistry.gov.uk. There are regional phone numbers listed on this site.

Pay stamp duty land tax

- **Stamp duty land tax** (SDLT) replaced stamp duty in December 2003, and is now the responsibility of the property owner who can, if they wish, ask their legal firm to deal with it (they'll charge about £50 for this service). If you agree a fixed fee for your conveyancing, as a lot of people do now, this may well be included as part of that service.

- It entails filling in a land transaction return form called SDLT1, available online or by post from the Inland Revenue (see box at foot of page, opposite).

- You or your legal firm can complete the form, and you have to sign it because you (not your representative) are held responsible if any of the information in it is wrong.

- Send it to the Inland Revenue together with your payment. No payment is required on properties sold for up to £125,000. After that, the rates are as outlined below.

- The Inland Revenue then issue you (or your legal firm, if you choose) with a certificate. This must be passed on to the Land Registry (also see box opposite) so that you can be registered as the owner of the property.

- The completed form and payment must be submitted within 30 days of the date of completion (date of settlement in Scotland), or you are liable for a £100 fine.

Stamp duty land tax charges

As of spring 2006, the current stamp duty rates are:

Selling price	Stamp duty land tax charge
Up to £125,000	Nil
£125,001–£250,000	1%
£250,001–£500,000	3%
£500,001 and above	4%

MAINTENANCE

Do bear in mind that all property requires maintenance. The survey or home condition report in the HIP (see pages 106–7) should identify any work that needs doing in the near future. If you didn't need one this time around, then you will when you sell the property (from June 2007). The surveyor should be able to advise you what needs doing and perhaps recommend a tradesman. Alternatively, go to the relevant tradesman organisation, such as the **Federation of Master Builders** (FMB) or the **NICEIC**. Whatever work you arrange, note it and keep the guarantees, warranties or safety certificates in your HIP. If you can't produce them for things like electrical work, you could have to get it done again.

If you've become a property owner for the first time, it is sensible to make a will or amend your existing one to help deal with your estate if you die.

The FMB website is www.fmb.org.uk and for the NICEIC, contact www.niceic.org.uk. For other help on tradesman institutions and organisations go to www.trustmark.org.uk and www.designsonproperty.co.uk.

Dealing with disputes

Mistakes can happen and problems can arise when dealing with anyone. There are generally ways around mishaps, but if the matter becomes more serious you need to know what procedures to follow. Read on for such information.

A lot of things can go wrong in the process of buying and selling property. Much of the time these problems are caused by lack of communication or preparation. The process also tends to bring out the worst in people: sellers and buyers can be greedy and may try to change the terms to get a better deal. Sometimes the professionals get caught up in this, and, of course, sometimes they make mistakes or don't behave to the highest standards. If you want to make a complaint about any of the services you received, follow these rules:

- **Be clear** about what went wrong and what you want done about it – do you want an apology, a reduced charge, or compensation?
- **Follow the organisation's** complaints procedure. This is most likely to begin with you explaining the complaint in writing to the people who did the work. If they do not deal with it to your satisfaction, go further up their organisation. If you're still not happy, go to their regulatory body or to an Ombudsman, if they are a member of one.
- **Keep copies** of all correspondence and notes of phone calls, including who you spoke to and when.
- **Be firm** but polite.
- **Set reasonable deadlines** for a response to your complaint.

> **❝ Sellers and buyers can be greedy and may try to get a better deal. The professionals can get caught up in this or make their own mistakes. ❞**

Organisations that help and advise on complaints include www.tradingstandards.gov.uk, www.citizensadvice.org.uk and www.which.net/aboutus/products/legal.html and www.howtocomplain.com.

All of the firms you deal with will be aware that you could be a future customer, and that many people ask their friends for recommendations, so it will be in their interest to deal with your complaint.

If you have a dispute with your HIP provider, you will need to go to their regulatory or trade body: RICS for surveyors, the Law Society for legal representatives, and the NAEA or OEA for estate agents, assuming they are members – see the box, below.

❝ The 'Move It' campaign on ww.which.co.uk provides templates of standard letters dealing with a variety of complaints against estate agents. ❞

DISPUTES WITH YOUR ESTATE AGENT

The most common complaint against estate agents is about their charges. You may feel these do not match the level of service you received, or you may get a nasty surprise when you see the bill. Check the wording of the contract you signed against the terms explained on pages 100–1. If there are extra charges on top of the fee, check if the contract alerted you to them.

If the charges reflect what is stated in the contract it is unlikely you have grounds to complain, but there is never any harm in laying out what you feel the company has done wrong and that you would like to have it put right. If they belong to a governing body (see box, below opposite), then they may be able to advise you.

You may have other complaints about the service you received. Did the agent check your buyer's financial credibility? Was their market valuation accurate – if the property sold very fast you were either lucky or underpriced. If it took a long time or you had to drop the asking price, maybe they – and you – were too ambitious. However, if you went against their advice in opting for a

 If your agent is a member of these organisations, you can complain to them if you aren't satisfied after raising the matter with the agent: National Association of Estate Agents (www.naea.org.uk) and the Ombudsman for Estate Agents (www.oea.co.uk).

very high asking price, you can hardly complain now. Were the sales particulars accurate? Did they pass on offers in writing or just on the phone (all offers should be communicated in writing)? Were they efficient in handling viewers' appointments and queries? These are all complaints about the service you paid for. If you feel it was poor, note this on the file and don't use them again or recommend them.

The website www.which.co.uk provides advice for dealing with a variety of complaints made against estate agents.

DISPUTES WITH YOUR SURVEYOR

If you were selling and had a HIP produced, you would have employed someone to do the home condition report (see pages 106–7). As a buyer, you may well have paid for a survey on the property you purchased.

If you discover a serious problem with the structure, damp or dry rot, read the survey and check if it was identified. If it wasn't, contact the surveyor and ask them to visit. If they agree there is a fault that isn't in

their report, or that they didn't indicate needed further investigation or was exempt from their survey, they should offer to compensate you, ideally by fixing the problem. They may argue that they did not have access to the area where the fault was apparent (the survey report is likely to have a clause explaining that the inspection cannot include difficult to access areas, such as under nailed down carpets or attics with no ladder). If so, ask if they have a 'hidden defects' policy. This covers the surveyor in such a situation.

All members of the Royal Institution of Chartered Surveyors (RICS) are part of its arbitration scheme. A trained arbitrator studies submissions by both parties and examines the evidence, sometimes including a visit to the property. If you choose to use it, you will have to pay £100 plus VAT.

DISPUTES WITH YOUR LEGAL FIRM

If you are surprised by any extra charges in your legal bill, check your original estimate. Sometimes these do not include search fees or electronic bank transfers. Other grounds for

Further contacts for redress are Royal Institution of Chartered Surveyors (www.rics.org.uk). You can also get details on the arbitration scheme from contactsrics@rics.org, tel: 0870 333 1600.

complaint are usually the speed of work and the quality of communication. These should not be issues if you followed the advice on selecting a legal firm on page 109 and managing the chain on pages 157–61, but if they are, follow the firm's

complaints procedure. It is worth asking the legal firm at the outset how long the conveyancing is likely to take, and for warnings of any delays.

To make a complaint about legal work, you must start by writing to the person who was responsible for it. If that doesn't work, go to the firm's complaints officer. The third stage is the complaints service of the Law Society where the firm is based: England and Wales, Scotland or Northern Ireland. If you are still

> ## "One of the solicitors tried to blame everyone else for not exchanging – but he got caught. "

Case Study   Mr and Mrs Bassett

Most of the complaints you hear about are to do with estate agents or, indeed, surveyors who may have missed something when checking a property. However, one of the professions whose errors are not always well publicised is the legal profession. Most do a good job, but in this instance, one of the solicitors tried to blame everyone else for not exchanging – but got caught!

In this case, a first-time buyer was buying a property, and the vendor of this property buying another. The second property being sold was the last one in the 'chain' as the couple (Mr and Mrs Bassett) were moving into rented

accommodation. So there were just two agents, three solicitors and a surveyor involved.

This short chain should have exchanged within weeks, but just at the last minute there was a problem in that one of the solicitors had apparently forgotten to request more documents for a vendor.

Becoming suspicious over what was happening, Mr and Mrs Bassett decided to find out what was holding up the exchange. They rang their solicitor to find out where the problem was. He spoke to the buyer's solicitor and was told they were ready to exchange, but were being held up by the first-time buyer's solicitor. Angry at this, the Bassetts rang

the agent who was selling the first property and asked if they could speak to the first-time buyer's solicitor to speed them up. A slightly confused estate agent rang back quickly to say that she had been told the reason for exchange was not the first-time buyer's solicitor, but that the middle solicitor was blaming them for the hold-up!

It soon became apparent that the solicitor who was the only one handling a sale and purchase was blaming the others for not being ready. The exchange was then concluded a few hours later after an ultimatum was sent. As there was no financial loss incurred, no further action was taken.

unhappy you can go to an ombudsman: The Legal Services Ombudsman in England and Wales, or the Scottish Legal Services Ombudsman, or the Lay Observer in Northern Ireland (see box, below).

If you have lost money due to poor conveyancing (perhaps by not being able to move into a property, or suffered an unreasonable delay caused by your solicitor), you may have a claim for negligence. This will initially be dealt with by the relevant law society (see box, below), but will eventually require the services of a solicitor to sue your provider.

DISPUTES WITH YOUR SELLER

If you find some fixtures or fittings that were supposed to stay have been removed, or vice versa, inform your solicitor and check they will deal with this as part of the service. They may

> ❝ If you have suffered financial loss because of poor conveyancing you may be able to claim. ❞

be able to help, but, sadly you have little practical comeback once the property has changed hands, and it is probably only worth the trouble if you feel very strongly about it.

DISPUTES WITH YOUR REMOVALS FIRM

There are some terrible horror stories about items being lost or damaged during a move or while they were in storage. Such incidents can be very upsetting because precious possessions have emotional as well as a financial value. If you used a reputable firm that is a member of a trade association or the removals ombudsman scheme (see box, below), the chances are all went well, and if it didn't, at least you've got someone to complain to who can help.

If the company doesn't create an inventory as part of the service, it's sensible to create one yourself. Try to get a representative of the company to sign it as this will help if there is a dispute at any point over what was on board the removal lorry.

Keep a written note of anything being broken or damaged during the move and ask the foreman to sign it.

Relevant legal websites are: www.theclc.gov.uk (Council for Licensed Conveyancers); www.lawsociety.org.uk (for England and Wales); www.lawscot.org.uk (for Scotland); www.lawsoc-ni.org (for Northern Ireland); www.lawsociety.ie (for Ireland); www.olso.org (legal services ombudsman); www.slso.org.uk (Scottish legal services ombudsman); www.adrnow.org.uk (Northern Ireland lay observer) and 03531 662 0547 (Independent adjudicator of the Law Society in Ireland).

Of course, you might not notice such events at the time, but aim to unpack as soon as you can and list anything that is broken or damaged as you find it. Take photographs of damaged goods as further evidence, particularly if you believe they were poorly packed. Immediately contact the firm and the insurers to inform them that you will be making a claim. Keep receipts for repairs or replacements to support your claim.

You might be offered a small sum in compensation on the grounds that the goods were used. Some firms also have a limit on how much you can claim per item – check this at the time of booking (see page 167) and also the basis on which they will replace/pay for damaged items – will it be new for old or like for like?

If you don't feel you are being offered enough, say so. It may be that you are covered by your insurance firm, too, so check with them what the situation is and if they will pay out or help you to recover monies from the removal company.

MAKING CLAIMS

If you discover that work such as timber treatment or damp proofing is faulty, check in the HIP or your paperwork for any guarantee.

If the firm has since gone out of business (sadly very common), it's not worth the paper it is written on. However, the Guarantee Protection Insurance Company provides insurance cover in specialist areas of building, and insures work done by members of the British Wood Preserving and Damp-proofing Association (BWPDA) so check if the firm were or are members. There is information about the ten-year warranty offered on new properties on page 130.

It is also worth checking that any guarantee is transferable to future purchasers of the property and isn't just for the benefit of the owner that had the work done.

However, it's only been since 31 March 2003 that free guarantees have been legally enforceable. So even if the company is still trading and the guarantee is transferable, if the company refuses to honour a free guarantee (issued before this date), then there may be little in practice you can do about it. The exception is Scotland, where even prior to this date a promise was legally enforceable.

 Websites for organisations who regulate removals firms are: www.bar.co.uk (British Association of Removers) and www.removalsombudsman.org.uk. For the Guarantee Protection Insurance Company go to www.gptprotection.co.uk and for the British Wood Preserving and Damp-proofing Association, go to www.bwpda.co.uk.

Selling and buying in Scotland

The property buying and selling process is different in Scotland and this chapter takes you through each stage explaining the differences. With a system based around binding bids, it is imperative that you thoroughly research the property you are interested in before handing over the envelope that could seal your fate.

Selling in Scotland

The residential property market in Scotland is worth about £16 billion annually. Each year there are more than 130,000 transactions and the average selling price has reached £126,538 as prices have risen substantially over the last few years.

The busiest market is the Glasgow area, but property costs are highest in the Lothian region (which includes historic Edinburgh) while the biggest price hikes at present are in the Highlands and Islands. More than a fifth of transactions are for cash with no mortgage involved. Just under a quarter of properties are purchased by first-time buyers – one of the lowest proportions in the UK. Because of the different system of buying and selling, the process is generally faster than south of the border.

Most property is sold through solicitors rather than estate agents. Groups of local solicitors often market properties for sale through a separate business called a '**property centre**', where all enquiries are passed on to the relevant solicitor. The property centres charge about £200 for this service, which runs for up to six months. Solicitors offer the same full marketing service as estate agents.

> **❝ Because of the different system of buying and selling in Scotland, the process is generally faster than south of the border. ❞**

They also produce their own property guide papers, called the *GSPC Property Guide* and *SSPC Guide*, which are fortnightly, full-colour listings of properties on the market, available at all property centres and many shops throughout Scotland.

Estate agents charge commission, which varies from 1.5 to 4 per cent of the selling price. Solicitors also work on commission and, in addition, will charge for the legal work involved, although it is quite common for them

The GSPC Property Guide is the largest property publication in Scotland. To find out more go to www.gspc.co.uk. Try also the Scottish Solicitors Property Centre (SSPC Guide) site at www.sspc.co.uk.

to set a single percentage fee for both of these services. Get several quotations from solicitors and estate agents so that you can make a comparison. Choose one who is a member of a professional association, and see the general advice on choosing estate agents and solicitors on pages 95–102 and 109, and in particular on reading the contracts carefully before agreeing to them (see page 100–2).

Jargon buster

Closing date Date by which sealed bids must be made

Entry date The same as a completion date in England and Wales

Fixed price A more definite price than the guideline price, which allows the possibility of a faster sale

Guideline price Guide for buyers on which offers are based. Also known as the 'upset price'

Property centre A group of local solicitors who market properties for sale

SETTING A PRICE

Your agent or solicitor will help you to decide the price, but you should also read the advice on researching your local market on pages 79–82. This is particularly important in a market such as Scotland where prices are rising and there are local and regional variations: different sectors can behave very differently, with some remaining static and others seeing significant uplift. When you have set a minimum and a maximum price, decide what the **guideline price** will be. This is the guide information for buyers, who will be expected to bid at least this figure, probably more. However, before they do this, the buyers will arrange a survey of the property – see the advice on getting your property ready and on dealing with viewings on pages 114–18.

You may decide it is in your interest to have your own property surveyed and make the report available to prospective buyers. The surveyor charges each party a small fee to look at the document, and charges the successful buyer the balance of the fee. You have to pay if you take the property off the market or if it has not sold after six months. This service is offered by www.surveysonline.co.uk. The advantage of this service is that buyers pay out less to get the

 Professional associations for estate agents and solicitors include the National Association of Estate Agents (www.naea.co.uk), the Ombudsman for Estate Agents (www.oea.co.uk) and the Law Society in Scotland (www.lawscot.org.uk).

The system of buying and selling property in Scotland is to undergo radical change in early 2008. New legislation will introduce a system called Purchaser's Information Packs (PIPs), which are similar to the HIP packs in England and Wales (see pages 105–8). The seller will become responsible for providing a survey with a home condition report and other information on the property, including local searches.

and this is known as the '**closing date**'. The bids will set a price and suggest an **entry date**, which is the same as a completion date. When you receive this information, read it carefully and discuss it with your adviser: the best price may not be the best bid. For example, a lower offer from a cash buyer or someone who wants an early completion date may be a better option, depending on your own circumstances.

Once you accept an offer you have a binding contract: if one of you changes your mind, you will have to pay compensation to the other party. So you don't need to worry about whether your buyer has their finances in place: they can't pull out.

> **❝ The system of buying and selling property is to undergo radical change in early 2008. ❞**

essential information, you get a chance to make any necessary repairs, and it is easier for people to post bids at the last minute. However, all of this will change in 2008 – see the box, above.

Your representative will set a time and date by which sealed bids must be made, usually noon on a weekday,

In a hurry?

If you need to move very quickly and haven't got time to go through the sealed bid process, or if your property has not attracted much interest, you could offer it at a **fixed price**. This allows you to market the property and accept the first offer you are happy with, which may be at that price or possibly below. This option can be useful if you need to act fast to clinch a purchase.

 Websites that give information on house prices in Scotland include: www.hbosplc.com; www.housepricescotland.com; www.myhouseprice.com; www.nationwide.co.uk and www.ros.gov.uk/citizen/index.html.

Buying in Scotland

It is just as important to be organised when buying property in Scotland as in any other part of the country. But bear in mind other matters.

The key differences when buying in Scotland as opposed to England or Wales are summarised below.

- **Properties are priced** at a guide level of the lowest acceptable price, and offers are always above this figure, sometimes by 30 per cent or more.
- **Buyers usually have surveys** done ahead of making an offer.
- **You need to have** your finances for the property organised prior to making an offer – i.e. a mortgage offer from a company.
- **Offers are typically** made 'blind' to a deadline – so you can't negotiate on price, and you need to be sure you can afford your offer. However, sometimes you can make an offer and have it accepted without going to a closing date.
- **Once an offer** has been accepted, you are committed to the purchase and will have to pay compensation if you pull out.
- **A moving date** is set once the offer is agreed, so there are fewer problems with managing chains.
- **Property is sold** on an owner-occupier basis: there is no **freehold** and very little **leasehold** property in Scotland.

Buying a property in Scotland is somewhat harder than selling one because of the expense of having a survey done on a property that you may not offer on or be successful in buying, plus the stress of making a sealed bid.

Start by reading the advice on pages 24–35 on working out what you can realistically afford. This is particularly important when buying in Scotland because if you make a successful bid but then can't raise the finance for it, you can be landed with a substantial demand for compensation. So do your figures, talk to a lender and get your MAP (see page 40). If you are also selling a property, get as far along the path with it as you can – being able to offer quick completion can be the difference between success and failure in the Scottish market.

❝ If you are also selling a property in the Scottish market, being able to offer quick completion can be the difference between success and failure. ❞

Stamp collecting

Include stamp duty land tax in your calculations of how much you can afford. The rates in Scotland are:

£125,001–£250,000	1%
£250,001–£500,000	3%
£500,001+	4%

There is also a fee for registering the title, charged on a sliding scale according to the price of the property you purchase.

CALL YOUR LAWYER

It is important to choose your solicitor before looking at homes. This will enable you to make an offer on a property with a tight deadline. Personal recommendation is one of the best ways to choose, but make sure your solicitor has experience in dealing with properties in the area and of the type that you are buying. You can also visit the Scottish branch of the Law Society on www.lawscot.co.uk to find suitable firms. If you are buying from outside Scotland, you will still need a Scottish solicitor, but your own solicitor may well have links with one.

As with any other service, find out what the costs and terms are – for example, if the fee includes stamp duty land tax, registration fees, expenses and VAT.

❝Make sure your solicitor has experience in dealing with properties in the area and of the type that you are buying.❞

LOOKING AT PROPERTIES

Once you have identified the likely areas where your preferred types of property exist (see pages 133–4), you can start looking at properties in your price range. The guideline price of properties on the market is geared to stimulate interest, and successful bids are likely to be at least 10 per cent higher – more in a rising market. So

Most solicitors' property centres and estate agents advertise in their own free newspaper and on websites. Some useful ones include: www.aspc.co.uk for the Aberdeen area; www.espc.co.uk for the Edinburgh area; www.gspc.co.uk for the Glasgow area and www.s1homes.com. You can also search on www.rightmove.co.uk.

do have a look at properties at a guideline price below your range: they may turn out to be what you want. Some sellers looking for a quick sale may put their property on at a 'fixed price' which is more like the asking price in England and Wales (see box on page 186), and new build properties are also priced in this way.

MULTIPLIED COSTS

A crucial difference between property purchase in England and Scotland is that north of the border offers are binding. That means you will need to have a survey done before you can make a realistic bid – so you have to spend some cash on finding out the condition of the property in order to decide if you even want to make an offer on it. There are two ways of avoiding this:

- Some sellers have a survey done themselves and interested buyers pay to view the document (see pages 185–6). This reduces the outlay considerably, and will also be the position when Purchaser's Information Packs become mandatory in 2008.
- You can make an offer 'subject to survey'. This is usually with the condition that your survey will be carried out very quickly (a deadline of one or two days is normal for

Case Study **Mr and Mrs Sim**

Mr and Mrs Sim currently live in a semi-detached property, which they had substantially extended two years ago. They were in a dilemma about taking the next step up the property ladder. Four-bedroomed detached properties in the area they liked offered little extra space (sometimes even offered less!), but they were keen to increase their property 'ownership'.

As luck would have it, the house next door became vacant when their neighbours relocated to England and after letting it out for 12 months, the previous owners mentioned that they intended to sell.

Having played around with the idea of buy-to-let for a few months previously, Mr and Mrs Sim saw this as the perfect opportunity to take the next step. They negotiated a private sale with their ex-neighbours, which went through extremely smoothly in about six weeks.

Despite one lender expressing concern about lending on the semi next door to their own house (because they feared the Sims would 'break through' to create one large detached property), Mr and Mrs Sim had managed to arrange the finance, organise a survey and successfully bid on the property.

So although they didn't get more space, they got a good investment in buy-to-let and will always ensure they keep good neighbours next door. The whole process was smooth, partly because of the system in Scotland where once an offer is accepted this means that you also exchange simultaneously.

this). If the seller accepts this, have the survey done independently and not through your lender, because they are unlikely to act with the speed you need. You can have three types of survey, the valuation from a mortgage lender, the homebuyer or the buildings survey (see pages 152–3 for more information).

If neither of these is possible and you are serious about the property, you'll need to commission your own survey. The fact that you could end up paying for several surveys before making a successful bid is known as the 'multiple survey' problem and is a recognised weakness of the Scottish property system, which will be addressed by PIPs. There is advice on reading and dealing with surveys on page 121, but in the Scottish system it is even more important to get a valuation from the surveyor (who should know the market very well) as

you have to make your offer with the full knowledge of estimates on any necessary repairs. If you are not still convinced you want the property, walk away.

MAKING AN OFFER

This is the really tricky bit because you only get one shot at it. The survey will brief you on the condition of the property and the inspector who carried it out should be able to suggest a value for it. You may be able to make an offer straight away: ask your solicitor to contact his or her counterpart to find out if you can. If not, they should 'note' your interest. This means that if another party expresses interest in the property you can be kept informed of this. A closing date is likely to be fixed for the bids, but this is not guaranteed: it is quite common for vendors to accept offers and agree the deal ahead of the closing date.

Factors to consider when making an offer in Scotland

- What price did the surveyor value it at?
- What did similar properties sell for?
- Is there potential for extending or other changes that would add value?
- What fixtures and fittings are included?
- Is the local market rising, falling or static?

- Can you afford to offer more if you want to?
- If you are a cash buyer or have sold your property already, you will be more attractive to the vendor.
- What 'entry date' would suit the vendor best?
- Can you bear to go through all this again if your bid is rejected?

Offers are made as sealed bids and the vital information is the price offered and the suggested entry date, when you complete the purchase – sometimes this can be weeks but it is usually a few months ahead. Discuss this date with your solicitor, taking into consideration the progress of the sale of your own property. A seller may accept a lower bid if the transaction can be completed quickly – and reject a higher bid that will take too long. If your bid is rejected, all you can do is put it down to experience and pick up the property papers again – but do ask why you weren't successful as you may get some useful feedback.

AFTER A SUCCESSFUL BID

When a bid is accepted, the two solicitors negotiate the details of the contract, such as the fixtures and fittings (see page 111), and the date of completion. The letters between them are known as 'missives', and the equivalent of exchanging contracts in the English system is called 'concluding the missives' in Scotland. At that point you become responsible for the structure of the building, so you need to arrange insurance on it. The solicitor also checks the title and reports on an exact description of the property and any conditions that you must understand as the new owner. After that, the solicitor does the conveyancing and prepares the 'disposition': the document transferring ownership to you.

The setting of a moving-in date makes the property chain less prone to delays than in England and Wales, as everybody is working to an agreed, binding schedule. However if you are moving to Scotland from another country you will have two sets of solicitors and it is important to keep up communication with all parties. About two weeks before the entry date you will be asked to provide the money for the deposit, stamp duty and your solicitor's fees. Your lender should transfer the balance of the money one day ahead of the entry date, at which point you sign all the legal documents.

Jargon buster

Concluding the missives Scottish term for exchanging contracts
Disposition Document transferring ownership
Freehold Ownership of a property and the land it is situated on
Leasehold Ownership for a set period, most commonly applied to flats and other shared buildings
Multiple surveys When you end up paying for several surveys before making a successful bid

Help for those on low incomes

There is general advice on some common problems with arranging a loan on pages 59-61, including joint ownership. However, the following information is specific to Scotland. There are a number of schemes to help those on low incomes to buy property, which are outlined below.

RIGHT TO BUY

This scheme allows you to buy a property you are renting at a discount. You may qualify for this if you are a tenant of a housing association or housing management co-operative, or of the council or a water or sewerage authority. If your current tenancy began before 2 January 1989, you can buy at a discount of 32–60 per cent. If your tenancy began after then but has lasted at least ten years, the discount is lower.

HOMESTAKE

A scheme run by Communities Scotland designed to help first-time buyers and those on low incomes to purchase a majority share in a property, with the remainder held by a local housing association.

SHARED OWNERSHIP

This allows people to buy a 25, 50 or 75 per cent share in a house or flat owned by a housing association, usually a new-build development. They can increase their share while they live in it and pay rent. Shared ownership is offered by many housing associations and some private developers. Council and housing association tenants or those on their waiting lists are given priority.

> **"** Shared ownership is offered by many housing associations and some private developers. **"**

For information on Homestake, contact www.communitiesscotland.gov.uk; for the Scottish Federation of Housing Associations, contact www.sfha.co.uk; for housing advice, contact www.scotland.shelter.co.uk, and go to www.homes.co.uk (Homes Mobility and Exchange Service) for information on shared ownership in Scotland and England.

Selling and buying in Northern Ireland and Ireland

There are a number of differences between buying properties in England or Wales and Northern Ireland. If you are dealing south of the border in Ireland, the process and terms used are different again. This chapter puts you on the right track in both countries.

10

Northern Ireland

The Northern Ireland property market has witnessed a boom in recent years, and the average property price has risen to about £140,000. At 70 per cent, home ownership is historically higher than the UK average, as is the figure for the number of individuals who live in each home.

SELLING IN NORTHERN IRELAND

The process of selling property in Northern Ireland is the same as in England and Wales, except that Home Improvement Packs (see pages 105–8) will not be introduced in Northern Ireland and contracts are termed as 'accepted' rather than 'exchanged', as is the case in England and Wales, which helps increase certainty within the sales process.

Whose land is it anyway?

There is a long history of confusion about ground rent on properties in Northern Ireland: in some cases, several people can claim to be due ground rent on the same land. To deal with this, purchasers of a property must now redeem any ground rent on it, turning it into a freehold, before they can register ownership with the Land Registry. This legislation does not apply to flats. Your solicitor should be able to advise if this must be done. The cost for compulsory purchase is nine times the annual ground rent, paid as compensation to the freeholder, plus a fee to the Land Registry office and a fee to your solicitor for witnessing the statutory form GR1, obtainable from the Land Registers of Northern Ireland (www.lrni.gov.uk). A leaflet explaining the Ground Rents Acts is available on the Office of Law Reform website at www.olrni.gov.uk.

 For advice on housing, go to northernireland.shelter.org.uk; nihe.gov.uk, the website of the Northern Ireland housing executive and www.co-ownership.org, the website of NICHA, the regional body for shared ownership.

BUYING IN NORTHERN IRELAND

If you are buying property in Northern Ireland, however, there are a few things that differ from buying in England and Wales.

Stamp duty

The rates of stamp duty are the same as for England and Wales (see page 31) but stamp duty has been waived in certain areas on properties selling for less than £150,000 in a government bid to encourage property development. However, you will still need to provide the Stamp Duty Land Tax Return form in order for the property to be registered (see page 175).

Buying on a low income

There are a number of schemes to help buyers on a low income.

66 As in the rest of the UK, anyone can set up as an estate agent in Northern Ireland and no qualifications are required. 99

Co-ownership

The Northern Ireland Co-ownership Housing Association (NICHA) gives people a chance to part rent, part buy a home. The properties available are set within certain 'value limits' by local councils and do not include housing association residences. You can apply direct to the NICHA or through an estate agent. You will need to obtain a mortgage for 50 per cent of the purchase price of the property, and you can increase the proportion of the property that you own in steps of 12.5 per cent.

Right to buy

Housing association and housing executive tenants are usually permitted to buy their home after living in it for five years. Up to four people can buy together if they have been living there for 12 months. This is called the Statutory House Sales Scheme.

Estate agents

As in the rest of the UK, anyone can set up as an estate agent and no qualifications are required. However, members of the Royal Institution of Chartered Surveyors (RICS) and the National Association of Estate Agents (NAEA) are all covered by their

Websites to look at when searching for property in Northern Ireland include www.findaproperty.com, www.propertynews.com and www.rightmove.co.uk. See also using property price surveys on pages 75-9.

organisation's code of conduct (see page 98), and some agents are governed by the estate agents ombudsman scheme. Fees are negotiable but the typical rate is 1.5 per cent of the selling price. See pages 95–101 for advice on selecting an agent – they are also known as auctioneers.

The legal side

Only solicitors can carry out conveyancing in Northern Ireland. Fees vary widely and it is a competitive market. Some firms stick to a charge of 1 per cent of the selling price plus an hourly rate (all plus VAT), others have a different fee

> ❝ Most property sales are by 'private treaty' and some go to auction. There are also cases of buyers being invited to tender for a property in a sealed bid. ❞

The Home Charter Scheme

The Law Society of Northern Ireland operates a compulsory kitemark quality scheme for solicitors. It sets minimum standards for typical tasks, providing a benchmark against which complaints can be measured. Go to www.lawsoc-ni.org for more information.

structure. Ask for a written estimate of their costs, including tax, registration, search and other expenses, so that you can make a proper comparison.

Most property sales are by 'private treaty' (see page 198) and some go to auction (see page 202). There are also cases of buyers being invited to tender for a property in a sealed bid, as in Scotland (see page 186).

Get it surveyed

As the HIPs won't be introduced to Northern Ireland, it is essential to commission an independent survey of the property – see pages 152–3 for advice on this.

New build

The average price of a newly built home in Northern Ireland is £116,000 and about 15,000 are built each year, of which just under a third are detached properties (see advice on buying new-build properties on pages 127–9). There are several guarantee schemes run by developers of new properties, including those run by the Construction Employers Federation (www.cefni.co.uk), the National House Building Council (NHBC) (www.nhbc.co.uk) and the Zurich Building Guarantee (www.zurich.co.uk).

Ireland

The Irish property market witnessed a boom in the 1990s, and while growth has since slowed, the market is still very active. Total dealings in 2005 reached 222,000.

Much of the growth was fuelled by a concerted burst of new building (recent years have seen upwards of 75,000 new builds per year – proportionately the highest building rate in Europe, and mostly privately funded). New homes are particularly attractive because buyers do not have to pay stamp duty unless the home covers more than 125 square metres (1,346 square feet). Other new-build incentives have been cut and demand for second-hand properties is now on the increase. In a hectic market there was growing public disquiet about practices such as setting prices too low at auction and a rise in gazumping, which the government is seeking to address.

SELLING IN IRELAND

The process of selling property in Ireland is similar to that in Scotland, in that once you sign the contract you are committed to the purchase or you will lose your deposit (see overleaf). Appoint your legal firm early on to give them time to collect your title deeds, making delays less likely later on. Estate agents in Ireland are often referred to as auctioneers because they have to hold either an Auctioneer's Licence or a House Agent's Licence. In fact, about a tenth of property sales are through auction houses.

In both cases, your representative should set an advised minimum value (AMV). This means the same as the asking price but has been introduced because a practice had developed of

> **❝In a hectic market there was growing public disquiet about practices such as setting prices too low at auction and a rise in gazumping. ❞**

 When you are looking to buy or sell in a growing market, there are different strategies to be borne in mind to when the market is falling. See pages 119 and 154 for advice on how to plan for each eventuality.

Any gazumping that occurs in Ireland is now mostly with builders acting through estate agents. Would-be purchasers who bought off plans, paid depostis and are waiting to sign contracts are, in some cases, being told that the contracts are ready for signing but that the price has gone up. The offer is pay the extra or get your deposit back – take it or leave it!

The reverse – gazundering – would only really happen in a depressed market where the buyer would delay signing the contract until the price was reduced further below that which was originally agreed.

If the property is your family home, you will be asked to sign a document proving that both partners are willing to sell it. This is a legal requirement under the Family Home Protection Act.

deliberately under valuing properties to generate more interest in them. Members of the Irish Auctioneers and Valuers Institute (IAVI) – who between them handle more than 85 per cent of property transactions in the country – must follow its code of conduct and employ this method.

Selling by private treaty

This is a contract that commits both parties to the sale and your buyer will lose the deposit if they pull out of the deal. Obviously you have to be totally committed to selling your home before signing it.

BUYING IN IRELAND

The Irish property market has seen major growth in the last decade with the total housing stock rising by nearly 50 per cent. However, this may be set to slow as the government has ended a major house-building incentive scheme and grants to first-time buyers, and begun instead to set levies on new homes. Demand remains high due to population growth (which is currently just over 4 million), immigration and high employment rates. Local authorities are able to require developers building five or more houses to set aside up to 20 per cent of the stock for social or affordable housing.

To get the most up-to-date information on Sterling–Euro conversions, see the website www.xe.com. It is worth checking the conversion rate regularly as markets fluctuate all the time.

Stamp duty land tax on property bought in Ireland

Selling price	First-time buyers	Others
€127,000–€190,500	None	3%
€190,501–€254,000	None	4%
€254,001–€317,000	None	5%
€317,001–€381,000	3%	6%
€381,001–€635,000	6%	7%
Over €635,001	9%	9%

Financing a purchase with a mortgage

As always, the first step is to decide what you can genuinely afford (see the guidance on pages 24–35). Remember to include the 'hidden costs' such as stamp duty (see box, opposite) and legal fees. From the stamp duty table you will see there are considerable advantages to being a first-time buyer in Ireland. Stamp duty does not apply on properties selling for less than €127,000. It is also not imposed on new houses up to the size of 125 square metres (1,346 square feet).

We agree, you pay a fee

Irish banks and building societies typically charge around 0.5 per cent of the value of a loan as an application fee. So a €150,000 loan would cost €750 to arrange. However, some waive this fee and you should always check the position before signing the agreement.

❝ With a rise in population growth, and immigration and employment rates, demand for property remains high in Ireland. ❞

The contact details for the Law Society of Ireland are: www.lawsociety.ie or telephone 03531 672 4800. Through the Law Society you will be able to contact reputable firms with which to deal.

Land Registry fees are charged on a scale from €125 to €625 depending on the property price. Total legal fees are likely to be 1–2 per cent of the purchase price. These fees are negotiable and it could pay to shop around among recommended firms. Always use a member of the Law Society of Ireland (see box, below). Deposits of 8–10 per cent of the selling price are also usually required, although some lenders are now offering 100 per cent mortgages. The typical loan term was 20 years but is subject to upward pressure as property prices rise.

Help for those on low incomes

There are a number of schemes in Ireland designed to help those on low incomes onto the property ladder.

Rent a Room

This is a government-run scheme allowing owner occupiers to rent out a spare room for up to €7,618 a year free of tax. You'll need to tell your mortgage company you intend to do this. This scheme could give your finances the kick-start they need, and, of course, you'll need to look for properties with at least two bedrooms.

The Affordable Housing Scheme

Here is a scheme that allows house buyers the chance to buy newly constructed homes and apartments in certain areas at a lower price.

Shared ownership

Shared ownership is a scheme in which you buy a proportion of your home, sharing its cost with the local authority. The property can be newly built or an existing house.

Local authority mortgages

Some local authorities offer loans up to a maximum of €165,000 to people who cannot get a mortgage from a building society or bank.

The Mortgage Allowance Scheme

This is for tenants of local authorities or housing associations. It offers up to €11,450 to reduce your mortgage payments during the first five years of the loan.

Housing co-operatives

The National Association of Building Co-operatives (NABCo) (www.nabco.ie) represents the co-operative housing movement in Ireland. It works in partnership with local authorities and private developers to provide homes in Ireland.

❝Estate agents in Ireland will tell you the advised minimum value (AMV) of properties. This is like the asking price in Northern Ireland.❞

Buying a home

See the advice on pages 124–45 on deciding what you need and want, researching the local market and choosing what to view. Estate agents in Ireland will tell you the advised minimum value (AMV) of properties. This is like the asking price in Northern Ireland (see pages 197–8). It has only recently come into use, superseding the guide prices that were generally set very low to maximise interest in the property. This led to much confusion and resentment as properties often sold at prices well above the initial guide price and beyond the means of some who had taken the trouble to view them.

New builds

There has been a boom in building new properties in Ireland in recent years, partly fuelled by the non-imposition of stamp duty on new properties under a certain size. There have been many expressions of concern about the standard of construction and finishing – it is said that the key worker on some sites is the decorator who can conceal the flawed work of the other tradesmen! Wooden framed (as opposed to cement block construction) houses have become more popular, partly because they are quicker to build. Read the advice on buying newly built properties on pages 127–9, and see the box, below, with information on guarantees.

Irish estate agent professional bodies are the Irish Auctioneers and Valuers Institute, which represents qualified auctioneers, estate agents, valuers and other property professionals (www.iavi.ie), and the Institute of Professional Auctioneers and Valuers, which represents and trains auctioneers and valuers (www.ipav.ie). The professional body for chartered surveyors in Ireland is the Society of Chartered Surveyors, www.scs.ie.

Selling and buying in Northern Ireland and Ireland

The fast pace of the market has led to many new-build houses being sold ahead of construction on the strength of the brochure. While this can give you more say on customising the house to your requirements (for example, placement of lighting and sockets and style of decoration), there is a risk of the project overrunning and the house not being completed in time – which can be a massive problem if you are part of a chain. Negotiate a moving-in date at the time you agree a deal.

Reduced government support has slackened the pace of new build and stimulated interest in second-hand properties and buying to renovate.

Contract or auction?

Slightly less than 10 per cent of Irish properties are sold at auction. This is always a risky business as you have to check out the property (at no little expense) in advance and then you can get sucked into bidding more than you wanted to at the auction before the gavel falls and you are faced with a demand for the deposit (see the advice on buying through auctions on page 137). The introduction of AMVs should end what seems to have been a widespread practice of under valuing properties to fill the auction floor with interested buyers. Do get your legal firm to check the contract for the property in advance, and do have a survey undertaken if you are serious about buying. Remember also that vendors are often happy to consider offers made ahead of the auction,

❝ The widespread practice of under valuing properties to fill the auction floor with interested buyers should end with the introduction of AMVs. ❞

Freehold or leasehold?

Property in Ireland can be freehold or leasehold. However, most leaseholders have the right to compulsorily buy the freehold title, which is worth doing as it makes the legal position more straightforward and therefore the property is easier to sell.

 AMV stands for advised minimum value. Other acronyms you might come across when dealing with property in Ireland are IAVI (Irish Auctioneers and Valuers Institute) and NABCo (National Association of Building Co-operatives).

One issue that used to affect buying property in Ireland was the number of illegal dumps. This is not really a problem any more as a system of waste disposal and charges has been introduced which places a heavy burden on anyone who would flaunt it. Anyone who comes across any illegal dumping or uncleared sites is encouraged to report it to the local authority.

spouses, which prevents one from selling the home without the agreement of the other.

Get a survey done

There is no HIP system proposed for Ireland, and as with all purchases, the message is 'buyer beware'. You should commission your own independent survey of the property to check for any flaws. The survey often pays for itself in financial terms as it can lead to re-negotiation of the price to allow for repairs, but it also has enormous value in peace of mind: you know what you are buying. Do not rely on your lender's valuation-only survey: there is advice on the other two types of survey on pages 152–3. Surveys cost between €120 and €380.

which can save a lot of heartache and hassle for both parties.

Most property in Ireland is sold by 'private treaty' (the equivalent of a contract that goes to exchange and completion in England and Wales) with a 'contract for sale' being signed after a price has been agreed. A deposit (usually 10 per cent of the selling price) is paid when this is signed, and lost if you pull out. The contract sets a completion date on which the balance must be paid. Legal queries are dealt with in the intervening period, which can be a slow business and is why there is a great potential for gazumping in Ireland (see the box on page 198).

One important check for a family residence property is that there is a declaration of consent from both

Glossary

AMV: Advised minimum value, the phrase for the lowest acceptable price in Ireland.

APR: Annual percentage rate, the figure that shows the true cost of the loan (or mortgage).

Asking price: Price at which a property is marketed.

Balance outstanding: The amount of a loan still owed.

Base rate: Interest rate set by the Bank of England, which is the rate at which banks can borrow money from the Bank of England, and is therefore what the banks use to set their interest rates.

Bridging loan: A loan allowing you to buy a property before finalising the sale of another property.

Building regulations: Standards of build set for new buildings, extensions and renovations.

Buildings insurance: The insurance on the structure of a property.

Buy to let: Purchasing a property to rent out to tenants.

Buying off plan: Purchasing an un-built new property from the plans.

BBR: Bank of England base rate (see above).

Capital: The initial mortgage loan.

Capital gains tax: Tax on profit from selling certain assets, not including your main place of residence.

CH: Central heating.

Chain: The series of people linked by related property sales and purchases.

Commission: A fee based on a percentage of the selling or purchase price; can apply to an independent financial adviser as well as an estate agent.

Commonhold: A recently introduced form of tenure offering an alternative to leasehold agreements.

Completion: The final part of the transaction when the transfer of the property title is legally given to the new owner.

Conditions of sale: The detailed standard terms governing the duties and rights of the buyer and seller.

Contract: The agreement to sell or purchase.

Covenant: A promise in a deed to do (or not do) certain things.

Conveyancing: The legal and administrative process of transferring ownership of land and/or property.

Deeds: The documents confirming ownership of property. Also known as title deeds.

Deposit: The down payment on a property, paid when contracts are exchanged.

DG: Double-glazing.

Disbursements: Costs incurred during the conveyancing process, which will be charged to the client.

Early redemption: Paying off a loan earlier than its term.

e-conveyancing: Carrying out conveyancing through web and email as well as over the phone.

Endowment mortgage: A loan where you only pay off the interest, linked to an endowment investment policy designed to pay off the sum borrowed at the end of the term.

Equity: The difference between the price of a property sold and the loan on it.

Exchange of contracts: A binding legal agreement that confirms the intention to transfer ownership of a property between a buyer and seller.

Final sale price: The agreed price of a property that is finalised at the time of exchange.

Fixtures and fittings: The term for the items attached to or part of a property, such as doors and light switches.

Freehold: Ownership of a property and the land it is situated on.

FSA: The Financial Services Authority.

Gazumping: When another person's (higher) offer is accepted, after a lower offer has already been accepted, but not become legally binding (i.e. before exchange of contracts).

Gazundering: When a purchaser reduces their offer at a late stage in the buying process, such as on the day of exchange.

GFCH: Gas-fired central heating.

Ground rent: Payment by the leaseholder to the freeholder. Low sums are sometimes referred to as a peppercorn rent.

Guide price: The marketing price of a property in Scotland, usually lower than the final price.

Higher lending charge: Policy taken out by the lender (but usually paid for by you) to cover them if the borrower does not make payments.

HIP: Home Information Pack, mandatory in England and Wales from June 2007.

Home condition report: The survey element of a HIP.

IFA: Independent financial adviser.

Indemnity policy: Insurance to protect a property owner in a dispute over ownership or restrictive covenants.

Instruction: Telling an agent you want them to sell your property.

Interest-only mortgage: A loan where you only pay the interest on the amount borrowed over the term of the mortgage.

Intermediary: A finance company offering products from a number of providers.

Joint agency: When two agents are instructed.

Joint tenancy: When two people own a property together and if one dies it automatically passes to the other, irrespective of the will.

Land certificate: Certificate confirming ownership of a property, issued by the Land Registry.

Leasehold: Ownership for a set period, most commonly applied to flats and other shared buildings.

Licensed conveyancer: A specialist trained in transfer of property ownership.

Local searches: Information on planning and environmental matters obtained from the local authority.

Mortgage: A loan for which property is the collateral.

Mortgage Agreement in Principle (MAP): An outline agreement to provide a loan to a specified person.

Mortgage protection policy: Life insurance taken out by the borrower so that the loan is paid off if they die or are sick (although policies do vary).

Mortgage redemption penalty: The charge sometimes made by the lender if you pay off your mortgage early.

Mortgage roll number or reference number: The reference number identifying your loan to the lender, required to draw down your title deeds when selling.

Multiple agency: When you instruct more than two estate agencies.

Negative equity: When your mortgage loan is higher on the property than the price you could sell it for.

Office copy: The 'official' copy of an entry from the Land Registry.

Part exchange: An arrangement in which your current home is bought by a developer (or a company they outsource to) to free up your monies to purchase their home.

PIP: Purchaser's Information Pack, mandatory in Scotland from 2008.

Planning permission: The go-ahead from a local authority for large physical changes to a property, such as adding a porch or garage.

Property portal: Websites with properties from a variety of agents.

PVC: Plasticised polyvinyl chloride, the material used to make plastic window frames.

Repayment mortgage: Loan where you pay the interest and the sum borrowed off at the same time for an agreed period.

Restrictive covenant: Legal restriction on what can be done on a property or on land.

Retention: The withholding of part of a loan until structural faults are corrected.

Sales particulars: The information prepared to market a property.

Sealed bid: Making an offer in a sealed envelope by a set date and time.

Searches: See local searches.

Shared ownership: Scheme where a housing association helps in the purchase of a property.

Snagging: The process of spotting the defects on new building work.

Sole agency: When you only instruct one estate agent.

Stamp duty land tax: Tax paid when you buy property, calculated as a percentage of the price.

Subject to contract: When a sale has been agreed but contracts have not been exchanged. Using the phrase prevents an offer being interpreted as a binding agreement.

Subject to survey: An offer made with the proviso that it may be amended or withdrawn if the survey shows flaws in the property.

SDG: Secondary double-glazing.

Sum insured: The insured amount that will be paid in the event of a valid claim being made.

Surrender value: The amount received if a life insurance policy is terminated early.

Survey: A report on the condition of a property.

Tenants in common: When more than one person owns a property but each person's share forms part of their estate if they die.

Term insurance: A life insurance policy with a time limit, usually used to cover the length of a mortgage.

Tied agent: An agent who also represents a limited list of financial companies or is owned by a financial company.

Title deeds: The documents proving ownership of land.

Top-up mortgage: An additional mortgage when the first loan is not sufficient for your needs.

Under offer: The stage between having an offer accepted and exchanging contracts.

UPVC: Unplasticised polyvinyl chloride, the material used to make windowframes.

Vacant possession: When a property being sold has no one living in it.

Valuation: The price a mortgage lender thinks a property will sell for. A mortgage valuation is a check by the lender that the property is as described in your mortgage application and that if you default on payment, the mortgage company will be able to get their money back when they sell your property.

Variable rate: When the interest rate is not fixed and can go up or down.

Vendor: The seller.

Useful addresses

Association of British Insurers
51 Gresham Street
London EC2V 7HQ
Tel: 020 7600 3333
www.abi.org.uk

British Association of Removers (BAR)
Tangent House
62 Exchange Road
Watford
Hertfordshire WD18 0TG
Tel: 01923 699480
www.bar.co.uk

**The British Holiday & Home Parks
Association**
Chichester House
6 Pullman Court
Great Western Road
Gloucester GL1 3ND
Tel: none available
www.ukparks.com

**British Wood Preserving and
Damp-proofing Association**
1 Gleneagles House
Vernongate
Derby DE1 1UP
Tel: 01332 225100
www.bwpda.co.uk

Building Cost Information Service (BCIS)
3 Cadogan Gate
London SW1X 0AS
Tel: 020 7695 1500
www.bcis.co.uk

BuildStore Ltd
Scottish Self Build Visitor Centre
Nettlehill Road
Houstoun Ind Estate
Livingston EH54 5DB
Tel: 0870 870 9991
www.buildstore.co.uk

Communities Scotland
Thistle House
91 Haymarket Terrace
Edinburgh EH12 5HE
Tel: 0131 313 0044
www.communitiesscotland.gov.uk

Construction Employers Federation
143 Malone Road
Belfast BT9 6SU
Tel: 028 9087 7143
cefni.co.uk

**Council for Licensed Conveyancers
(CLC)**
16 Glebe Road
Chelmsford
Essex CM1 1QG
Tel: 01245 349599
www.theclc.gov.uk

Council of Mortgage Lenders (CML)
Council of Mortgage Lenders
3 Savile Row
London W1S 3PB
Tel: 020 7437 0075
www.cml.org.uk

Designs on Property
Pear Tree House
3a Church Street
Long Bennington
Newark NG23 5EN
Tel: 0845 838 1763
www.designsonproperty.co.uk

easier2move.co.uk
22–24 Clarence Street
Southend-on-Sea
Essex SS1 1BH
Tel: 07004 327437
www.easier2move.co.uk

Electrical Contractors' Association (ECA)
ESCA House
34 Palace Court
London W2 4HY
Tel: 020 7313 4800
www.eca.co.uk

English Heritage
PO Box 569
Swindon SN2 2YP
Tel: 0870 333 1181
www.english-heritage.org.uk

Environment Agency
Rio House
Waterside Drive
Aztec West
Almondsbury
Bristol BS32 4UD
Tel: 0870 8506 506
www.environment-agency.gov.uk.

ExCel London
One Western Gateway
Royal Victoria Dock
London E16 1XL
Tel: 020 7069 5000
www.excel-london.co.uk

Federation of Master Builders (FMB)
Gordon Fisher House
14–15 Great James Street
London WC1N 3DP
Tel: 020 7242 7583
www.fmb.org.uk

Financial Ombudsman Service
South Quay Plaza
183 Marsh Wall
London E14 9SR
Tel: 0845 080 1800
www.financialombudsman.org.uk

Financial Services Authority (FSA)
25 The North Colonnade
Canary Wharf
London E14 5HS
Tel: 020 7066 1000
www.fsa.gov.uk

Guarantee Protection Insurance Company (GPI)
27 London Road
High Wycombe
Bucks HP11 1BW
Tel: 01494 447010
www.gptprotection.co.uk

HBOS plc
PO Box No. 5
The Mound
Edinburgh EH1 1YZ
Tel: 0870 600 5000
www.hbosplc.com

Health Protection Agency
7th Floor
Holborn Gate
330 High Holborn
London WC1V 7PP
Tel: 020 7759 2700
Radon hotline: 01235 822622
www.hpa.org.uk/radiation/radon/index.htm

209

Homecheck
Imperial House
21–25 North Street
Bromley BR1 1SS
Tel: 0870 606 1700
www.homecheck.co.uk

Hometrack Data Systems Limited
2/10 Harbour Yard
Chelsea Harbour
London SW10 0XD
Tel: 0800 019 4440
www.hometrack.co.uk

Housing Corporation
Maple House
149 Tottenham Court Road
London W1T 7BN
Tel: 0845 230 7000
www.housingcorp.gov.uk

The Independent Park Home Advisory Service
17 Ashley Wood Park
Tarrant Keyneston
Blandford Forum
Dorset DT11 9JJ
Tel: none available
www.iphas.co.uk

Inspector Home
7 Station Road
Epping
Essex CM16 4HA
Tel: 0845 408 4979
www.inspectorhome.co.uk

Institute of Professional Auctioneers and Valuers
IPAV Headquarters
129 Lower Baggot Sreet
Dublin 2
Ireland
Tel: 03531 678 5685
www.ipav.ie

Irish Auctioneers and Valuers Institute
38 Merrion Square
Dublin 2
Ireland
Tel: 03531 661 1794
www.iavi.ie

LABC Services
137 Lupus Street
London SW1V 3HE
Tel: 020 7641 8737
www.labc-services.co.uk

Law Society of England and Wales
113 Chancery Lane
London WC2A 1PL
Tel: 020 7242 1222
www.lawsociety.org.uk

Law Society of Ireland
Blackhall Place
Dublin 7
Ireland
Tel: 03531 672 4800
www.lawsociety.ie

Law Society of Northern Ireland
Law Society House
98 Victoria Street
Belfast BT1 3JZ
Northern Ireland
Tel: 028 90 231614
www.lawsoc-ni.org

Law Society of Scotland
26 Drumsheugh Gardens
Edinburgh EH3 7YR
Tel: 0131 226 7411
www.lawscot.org.uk

Legal Services Ombudsman
3rd Floor
Sunlight House
Quay Street
Manchester
Tel: 0845 601 0794
www.olso.org

The Listed Property Owners Club
FREEPOST
Hartlip
Sittingbourne
Kent ME9 7TE
Tel:01795 844939
www.lpoc.co.uk/intro.htm

The NEC
Birmingham B40 1NT
Tel: 0870 730 0196
www.necgroup.co.uk/whatson/

National Association of Estate Agents (NAEA)
Arbon House
21 Jury Street
Warwick CV34 4EH
Tel: 01926 496800
www.naea.co.uk

National Federation of Builders (NFB)
55 Tufton Street
London SW1P 3QL
Tel: 0870 8989
www.builders.org.uk

National Guild of Removers and Storers
3 High Street
Chesham
Buckinghamshire HP5 1BG
Tel: 01494 792279
www.ngrs.co.uk

The National House Building Council (NHBC)
Buildmark House
Chiltern Avenue
Amersham HP6 5AP
Tel: 01494 735363
www.nhbc.co.uk

National Inspection Council for Electrical Installation Contracting (NICEIC)
Warwick House
Houghton Hall Park

Houghton Regis
Dunstable
Bedfordshire LU5 5ZX
Tel: 01582 531000
www.niceic.org.uk

The National Park Homes Council
Catherine House
Victoria Road
Aldershot
Hants GU11 1SS
Tel: 01252 318251
www.theparkhome.net

Northern Ireland Federation of Housing Associations
38 Hill Street
Belfast
BT1 2LB
Tel: 028 9023 0446
www.nifha.org

Northern Ireland Lay Observer
The Administrative Team
Advice Services Alliance
12th Floor, New London Bridge House
25 London Bridge Street
London SE1 9SG
Tel: 020 7378 6428
www.adrnow.org.uk

Office of the Deputy Prime Minister (ODPM)
Eland House
Bressenden Place
London SW1E 5DU
Tel: 020 7944 4400
www.odpm.gov.uk

Ombudsman for Estate Agents (OEA)
Beckett House
4 Bridge Street
Salisbury
Wilts SP1 2LX
Tel: 01722 333306
www.oea.co.uk

Post Office Ltd
Customer Care
FREEPOST NAT18105
Sunderland SR3 3BR
Tel: 08457 22 33 44
www.postoffice.co.uk

The Removals Industry Ombudsman
PO Box 771
Tring
Hertfordshire HP23 5XB
Tel: none available
www.removalsombudsman.org.uk

Royal Institution of Chartered
Surveyors (RICS)
Contact Centre
Surveyor Court
Westwood Way
Coventry CV4 8JE
Tel: 0870 333 1600
www.rics.org

Scottish Federation of Housing
Associations
38 York Place
Edinburgh
EH1 3HU
Tel: 0131 556 5777
www.sfha.co.uk

Scottish Legal Services Ombudsman
17 Waterloo Place
Edinburgh
EH1 3DL
Tel: 0131 556 9123
www.slso.org.uk

Shelter
88 Old Street
London EC1V 9HU
Tel: 020 7505 4699
www.shelter.england.co.uk

The Society of Chartered Surveyors
5 Wilton Place
Dublin 2
Ireland
Tel: 01676 5500
www.scs.ie

Surveys Online Ltd
OneSearch Direct
1st Floor
Skypark SP1
8 Elliot Place
Glasgow G3 8EP
Tel: 08700 855050
www.surveysonline.co.uk.

UpMyStreet
10th Floor
Portland House
Stag Place
London SW1E 5BH
Tel: 020 7802 2992
www.upmystreet.com/

Which?
Castlemead
Gascoyne Way
Hertford SG14 1LH
0845 307 4000 or 01992 822800
www.switchwithwhich.co.uk/mortgage
www.which.co.uk

Zurich Insurance
Southwood Crescent
Farnborough,
Hampshire GU14 0NJ
Tel: 0870 2418050
www.zurich.co.uk

Property websites

http://ukauctionlist.com
www.designsonproperty.co.uk
www.findaproperty.com
www.Fish4homes.co.uk
www.heritage.co.uk
www.houseprices.co.uk
www.houseweb.co.uk
www.myhouseprice.com
www.ourproperty.co.uk
www.periodproperty.co.uk
www.primelocation.com
www.propertybroker.co.uk
www.propertynews.com (for Northern Ireland and Ireland)
www.rightmove.co.uk
www.ruralpropertyindex.co.uk
www.ruralscene.co.uk

Websites dealing with property-related money issues

www.citizensadvice.org.uk (Citizens Advice Bureau – regional offices)
www.clsdirect.org.uk (Community Legal Service)
www.co-ownership.org (regional body for shared ownership)
www.direct.gov.uk (directory of public services)
www.hbosplc.com/economy/housingresearch.asp (Halifax house price index)
www.homes.org.uk (shared ownership information in Scotland and England)
www.housingcorp.co.uk (portal for housing related issues)
www.housinginwales.co.uk (housing news in Wales)
www.iammoving.com (change of address service)
www.landregistry.gov.uk (registers title to land in England and Wales)
www.lease-advice.org (Leasehold Advisory Service)
www.moneynet.co.uk (finance comparisons)
www.moneysupermarket.co.uk (finance comparisons)
www.nationaldebtline.co.uk (advice on dealing with debt problems)
www.nationwide.co.uk/hpi (Nationwide house price index)
www.planningportal.gov.uk (online planning resource)
www.propertybroker.co.uk (service for buying and selling property)
www.tradingstandards.gov.uk (consumer protection information)
www.whatmortgage.co.uk (mortgage broker)

Index

Index

MOVING HOUSE? – Switch with Which?

So you're moving house? Seize this opportunity to make radical cuts to your budget. Switch with Which? and save not just on your mortgage, but also your energy bills, your current account and your mobile phone. With the bewildering array of options available, it can be hard for consumers to compare their options, so use our switching sites to help you find the best deal for you.

Switch your mortgage

The mortgage market is very competitive and it makes sense to review your mortgage regularly to see whether you're getting the best deal. Our mortgage search is the only place that you can compare constantly updated details of over 8,000 mortgages and find out how much you can really save by switching.

Switch your mobile phone

Whether you're on pay as you go or contract, there are savings to be had. Our mobile tariff comparison is quick and easy to use, updated every month and completely independent. So why wait? Let us do the hard work, so you can start saving money.

Switch your energy supplier

Moving house can be a great time to switch gas or electricity supplier. Don't just settle for the existing supplier, choose the best deal for you. Since deregulation of the energy market, millions of households have saved money by switching energy suppliers, but if you've never switched, you could be wasting a lot of money. Our service enables you to search out the best deal and switch quickly and easily.

Switch your current account

Like to earn more interest when you're in credit, dramatically reduce the cost of your overdraft or get better service? Switching accounts is much easier than you think. As well as comparing rates and banking facilities for all UK current accounts, we've included our unique customer satisfaction data. And don't forget, the banks now do all the work of moving your direct debits and standing orders for you, making the switch even easier.

Switch with Which? provides consumers with an impartial source of information on essential services that affect every household.

So why not save money now by using www.switchwithwhich.co.uk?

Which? is the leading independent consumer champion in the UK.
A not-for-profit organisation, we exist to make individuals as powerful as the
organisations they deal with in everyday life. The next few pages give you a
taster of our many products and services. For more information, log onto
www.which.co.uk or call 0800 252 100.

Which? magazine

Which? is, quite simply, the most trusted magazine in the UK. It takes the stress
out of your buying decisions by offering independent, thoroughly researched advice
on consumer goods and services from cars to current accounts via coffee makers.
Its Best Buy recommendations are the gold standards in making sound and safe
purchases across the nation. Which? has been making things happen for all
consumers since 1957 – and you can join us by subscribing at www.which.co.uk
or calling 0800 252 100 and quoting 'Which'.

Which? online

www.which.co.uk gives you access to all Which? content online. Updated daily, you
can read hundreds of product reports and Best Buy recommendations, keep up to date
with Which? campaigns, compare products, use our financial planning tools and
interactive car-buying guide. You can also access all the reviews from the *The Which?
Good Food Guide*, ask an expert in our interactive forums, register for e-mail updates
and browse our online shop – so what are you waiting for? www.which.co.uk.

Which? Legal Service

The Which? Legal Service offers immediate access to first-class legal advice at
unrivalled value. One low-cost annual subscription allows members to enjoy
unlimited legal advice by telephone on a wide variety of legal topics, including
consumer law (problems with goods and services), employment law, holiday
problems, neighbour disputes and parking/speeding/clamping issues. Our qualified
lawyers help members reach the best outcome in a user-friendly way, guiding them
through each stage on a step-by-step basis. Call 0800 252 100 for more information
or visit www.which.co.uk.

Gardening Which?

If you're passionate about gardening, then you'll love *Gardening Which?* Every month, this informative and inspirational magazine brings you 70 pages of the best plants, products and techniques, all backed by expert research and stunning photography. Whatever type of gardener you are, we've got all the advice to make your life easier – and because it's published by Which? you know it's advice you can trust. To find out more about *Gardening Which?* log on to www.which.co.uk or call 0800 252 100 and quote 'Gardening'.

Holiday Which?

Full of independent and unbiased travel advice, *Holiday Which?* gives you the lowdown on insurance, tour operators and holiday health, as well as the know-how to avoid rip-offs and get compensation when it's due. That's not all – the magazine also contains information on the best short breaks, long-haul trips and fun days out, recommending good places to stay and eat. To find out more about *Holiday Which?* log on to www.which.co.uk or call 0800 252 100 and quote 'Holiday'.

Computing Which?

If you own a computer, are thinking of buying one or just want to keep abreast of the latest technology and keep up with your kids, there's one invaluable source of information you can turn to – *Computing Which?* magazine. *Computing Which?* offers you honest unbiased reviews on the best (and worst) new technology, invaluable problem-solving tips from the experts and step-by-step guides to help you make the most of your computer. To subscribe, call 0800 252 100 and quote 'Computing' or go to www.computingwhich.co.uk.

Which? Books

Which? Books provide impartial, expert advice on everyday matters from finance to law, property to major life events. We also publish the country's most trusted restaurant guide, *The Which? Good Food Guide.* To find out more about Which? Books, log on to www.which.co.uk or call 01903 828557.

Other books in this series

Which? Essential Guides
Buying Property Abroad

Jeremy Davies
ISBN: 1-84490-024-X/978-1844-900-244

A complete guide to the legal, financial and practical aspects of buying property abroad. This book provides down-to-earth advice on how the buying process differs from the UK, and how to negotiate contracts, commission surveys, and employ lawyers and architects. Practical tips on currency deals and taxes – and how to command the best rent – all ensure you can buy abroad with total peace of mind.

Which? Essential Guides
The Pension Handbook

Jonquil Lowe
ISBN: 1-844900-25-8/978-1844-900-251

A definitive guide to sorting out your pension, whether you're deliberating over SERPs/S2Ps, organising a personal pension or moving schemes. Cutting through confusion and dispelling apathy, Jonquil Lowe provides up-to-date advice on how to maximise your savings and provide for the future.

❝ Which? tackles the issues that really matter to consumers and gives you the advice and active support you need to buy the right products. ❞